Malcolm Marshall's
Bowling and Fielding Skills

Malcolm Marshall's
Bowling and Fielding Skills

A Complete Step-By-Step Guide

Specially commissioned photography by Action Plus

HAMLYN

Acknowledgements There are many people to thank for their help and co-operation in putting together this book. In particular I would like to thank Mike Taylor and Tony Baker at Hampshire CCC for allowing us to use the County Ground at Southampton for the photographic shoot and the groundsman, Nigel Gray, for preparing the strip. Thanks too to Bobby Parks and Tony Holmes for their help with batting and wicket-keeping during the session. Lastly many thanks to Peter Arnold who helped me to put my ideas into words and to Hampshire scorer Vic Isaacs for providing the statistical information.

Picture Acknowledgements Allsport:Adrian Murrell: 1, 2, 8 top, 21 top; C. Cole: 9 top; Ben Rutherford: 3 Colorsport: 15 right, 33 right, 35 left, 35 right, 38 bottom, 39 left, 39 right, 43 right, 63 left, 63 centre, 63 right; Patrick Eagar: 8 bottom, 9 bottom, 23 top, 23 bottom, 27 bottom, 28 top, 32, 33 left, 37, 41 top, 49 top, 55 bottom, 59; Hulton: 29 bottom; Sports Line: David Munden: Front Cover

First published in Great Britain in 1994 by Hamlyn an imprint of Reed Consumer Books Limited
Michelin House, 81 Fulham Road, London SW3 6RB
and Auckland, Melbourne, Singapore and Toronto

Copyright © 1994 Reed International Books Limited

ISBN 0 600 58269 8

A catalogue record for this book is available from the British Library

Project Editor: David Heslam, *Art Editor:* Bryan Dunn
Designed by: Vivien J McDonald – Vivitext Creative Services
Picture Research: Claire Taylor, *Production Controller:* Michelle Thomas

Printed and bound in Great Britain by
Butler & Tanner Ltd, Frome and London

Contents

Introduction

I WON'T say fast bowling came naturally to me, because right up until a year or two before my first Test match I regarded myself as a batsman, who at the same time was useful enough as a medium-pace change bowler to get a few wickets. As a matter of fact I still think of myself as an all-rounder, although of course it is being able to bowl fast which has made me successful as an international cricketer.

So perhaps the first tip I could give to any very young cricketer reading this book is this: do not make up your mind straightaway what sort of cricketer you want to be. Life might have some surprises in store. Just go out and play cricket, and enjoy whatever you happen to be doing: batting, bowling or fielding. You will discover in time what you are best at.

As it happens, I always wanted to be a wicket-keeper. David Murray, who kept wicket for the West Indies, came from the same district in Barbados as me, and I would have liked to have taken over from him in the West Indies side (he is eight years older than me). Sometimes I still wish I had, although as as luck would have it we did play in six Tests together.

Perhaps I liked being wicket-keeper because the 'keeper is always in the game. My great hero as a boy, though, was Garfield Sobers, another player from Bridgetown. I first saw him play in a Test match at Bridgetown in 1972, just before my 14th birthday. New Zealand had led West Indies by nearly 300 runs on the first innings, but Gary helped save the match with 142 in the second knock. From then on I turned my collar up like Sobers and even walked like him – and Clive Lloyd thinks I haven't got over it yet.

I played cricket from the time I could hold a homemade bat, and played on parks, wasteland, even in the streets, not letting a moment go to waste. I was not out of the ordinary as a player – perhaps partly because I was often playing with bigger and stronger boys. This no doubt toughened me up. Even at school I was still a batsman and wicket-keeper, and just about the smallest boy in the class.

Lunchtime matches in the school playground helped decide my fate as a bowler. Sometimes it took so long to get the other side out that you could go all week without batting. I decided that to get an innings I would have to get a few batsmen out myself.

Even as a reluctant bowler, it seems I had the shoulder action which has remained with me ever since. But it was still as a batsman that I began in competitive schools cricket – my first century came before any great success as a bowler. It was only when I began to play club cricket as a teenager that I gradually began to learn to bowl fast, and at 18 or so I realised I was good enough perhaps to make a living at cricket. Soon after getting into the Barbados side at 19, I was called up to tour India with a West Indian side weakened by the Packer affair and, still only 19, I took my first Test wicket.

This account might make it all sound easy and as if I had no help, but of course this is untrue. Top-class club cricketers and school teachers had taken an interest in my cricket ever since I showed promise, and men like Nolan Clarke and Maurice Morrison, to name but two, encouraged and helped me. Always before me as a fast bowler was the inspiration of the legendary Wes Hall, who also comes from Barbados, and indeed Barbados was teeming with outstanding cricketers.

Once I was in the West Indies side other famous players helped my development, and who could pick up tips from better players than Andy Roberts, Joel Garner and Michael Holding?

What my experience tells me most, however, is that the prime ingredients for success are enthusiasm and the determination to work hard. I have never lost my love of the game, and have never overlooked the need to keep fit and to train conscientiously.

I hope that in reading this book you will pick up a few technical pointers and tips that will benefit your game. But none of them will help if you are not determined to work.

Work at making your body strong. I am a firm believer as a fast bowler in the need to have strong abdominal muscles, and even now I do my sit-ups to keep them in trim. But all cricketers, not just fast bowlers, need to be fit and strong. You cannot use your body in spurts to play cricket without building it up between times.

Set yourself goals. For example, decide which club you would like to play for and set a time limit to make the team – say two years to get into the first team. Set a total of wickets you expect to get in the season. But do not be despondent if you fail. Keep going!

If you do succeed, don't let success go to your head. Remain the same person as you were before. Don't forget you can always get even better. Don't allow the big hope to become the big flop. Keep trying and progressing.

I wish you the best of luck, and hope you enjoy playing the game as much as I do.

Malcolm Marshall Factfile

Malcolm Marshall shows his delight at the sight of Graham Gooch's middle stump during the fourth Test at Edgbaston in 1991.

MALCOLM DENZIL MARSHALL was born in Bridgetown, Barbados on 18 April 1958. He was keen on cricket as a youngster, and made his debut for Barbados in the 1977-78 season. He played well, and with many West Indian players temporarily forfeiting their Test careers to play in Kerry Packer's World Series cricket, he was picked for West Indies' tour of India in 1978-79. He made his Test debut in the second Test and became a regular in the West Indies side in 1980.

Meanwhile, he took up a contract with Hampshire in 1979 which lasted until 1993. Marshall's value to Hampshire throughout the 1980s was highlighted by his efforts in 1982, when he took 134 wickets, easily the most wickets in a season taken by any bowler since the number of County Championship games had been reduced ten years earlier. His performances in 1982 made him one of Wisden's 'Five Cricketers of the Year' and he was voted almost unanimously by the county batsmen to be the fastest bowler on the circuit.

For the next ten years, Marshall was one of the best and most successful bowlers in the world. Not tall for a fast bowler (5ft 10½ in, or 1.79 m), his fitness, dedication and skill brought him 376 Test wickets, a West Indian record. When he took his 300th Test wicket (David Boon in 1988-89) his strike-rate of a wicket every 45.85 deliveries was the best of all bowlers with over 300 Test wickets. He also took his wickets cheaper than all the others in the '300 club', each wicket costing him only 20.94 runs.

However impressive they are, figures can only indicate a bowler's greatness – it is performances on the field which confirm it. Perhaps Marshall's best-remembered Test match was that at Headingley in 1984. After bowling only six overs

One of Malcolm Marshall's 376 Test victims. Paul Downton taken at third slip by Roger Harper at Old Trafford in 1988.

The sight that has unnerved batsmen all over the world.

Malcolm Marshall's Career Bowling Statistics
First Class Cricket

BOWLING:	Runs	Wkts	Avge	Best	5W	10wM
for Hampshire	15401	826	18.64	8-71	45	7
for Barbados	3146	180	17.47	6-38	8	1
for Natal	451	28	16.10	6-45	1	0
for other teams	2496	142	17.57	7-56	8	1
for West Indies	7876	376	20.94	7-22	22	4
TOTALS	29370	1552	18.92	8-71	84	13

Batting Statistics
First Class Cricket

BATTING:	Mat	Inns	No	Runs	HS	Avge	100s
for Hampshire	210	269	37	5847	117	25.20	5
for Barbados	37	49	7	1270	89	30.32	–
for Natal	5	8	0	87	35	10.87	8
for other teams	46	47	9	1099	109	28.92	1
for West Indies	81	107	11	1810	92	18.85	–
TOTALS	379	480	64	10113	117	24.31	6

on the first morning he suffered a double fracture of his left thumb, and retired from the field, being advised not to play again for at least ten days. However, with West Indies at 290 for nine, only 20 ahead, and with Gomes on 96, he came in at number 11 to bat one handed while Gomes completed his century and West Indies' lead reached 32. Then, with his hand heavily plastered, he achieved his best Test analysis till then by taking seven for 53 as West Indies won comfortably. Marshall always did well in England, and his best Test series came in 1988, when he took 35 wickets at the remarkably low cost of 12.65.

Off the pitch, Marshall is a happy, considerate person with a liking for reggae music and a good joke, but on the pitch he is dedicated to taking wickets, and has proved himself to be one of cricket's best-ever fast bowlers.

No need for Dickie Bird to raise his finger! Mike Gatting is comprehensively bowled by Malcolm Marshall in the 1988 Trent Bridge Test.

Getting Ready to Bowl

Y OU need to be fit to be a bowler, particularly a fast bowler, and of course all your fitness exercises – jogging, running, swimming, sit-ups, etc. – will have been done before the match, or indeed the season, starts. These pages deal with the loosening up exercises and routines before you actually come on to bowl.

First of all, though, you should ensure that you are well-dressed and comfortable. There is an old cricket saying that if you cannot be a cricketer you can at least look like one. Make sure your clothes are clean and fit well, and pay particular attention to your footwear. You cannot bowl properly if you are worried about your sleeves flapping or getting a blister on your foot. If you feel good and look good you'll bowl better.

Warm-up Exercises

I do some basic stretching exercises designed to get the blood to the muscles and to loosen up my body before I go on to bowl. In 1983 I was given the honour of regularly opening the bowling for the West Indies Test team, and since then I have usually opened the bowling for

1

Rotating my left arm in a circle, which I do forwards and backwards to loosen arm and shoulder muscles.

whatever team I play for, so my loosening up exercises are often done before the match starts. They are very simple.

I take great care of my back and abdominal muscles, and do plenty of sit-ups in my usual training – 150 a day perhaps in batches of tens. A sharp twinge in my back on the 1981–82 tour of Australia blew up into a serious back injury and I thought my touring days might be over before they had hardly begun. It took a lot of work with my friend Edmund Sealey, the physio to the Barbados athletics squad, to get me

1

With elbows bent and feet still I turn my head and body as far as it will go to my right.

2

I now turn my head and body to my left. I repeat ten or so times to loosen my back muscles.

2

I alternate rotating my left arm with my right, doing each backwards and forwards about ten times each way.

Marshall Law

■ Never forget your stretching exercises, particularly in the relatively cold, damp weather in which we often play in England. Muscles stretched and warmed up are much less likely to give way.
■ Ease into the stretching gently.
■ Occasionally repeat exercises while fielding to keep the muscles supple all day.

back to a level of fitness for cricket.

So I loosen up my torso by rotating my head and body from side to side, with elbows bent.

I get my arms and shoulders loose by rotating my arms backwards and forwards one at a time.

I stretch my thigh muscles by bending the knee and raising the foot behind me, grabbing the foot with my hand and gently pulling the foot to stretch the thigh. Alternate the exercise with both legs.

Hamstrings, too, are important. I loosen up mine by spreading my legs and then bending each knee in turn while pushing down on the other.

Don't forget to do the exercises gently, with co-ordination. Jumping into them too violently would defeat the purpose, since they are meant to ease you into the looseness needed for the all-out effort which will follow.

1

Gently pulling my left foot backwards to loosen the thigh muscles.

2

Repeating this action with the right leg. I do both about ten times alternately before bowling.

Basic Principles of Fast Bowling

BOWLERS can be the workhorses of cricket – sometimes there's a lot of work for little reward. But there's no better feeling then clean bowling a batsman – so although bowlers wait longer for their pleasures, they are sweeter when they come!

Bowling is not an automatic activity and bowlers always have to think about their game – how they can get more control, more accuracy, more speed, spin or swing – and they pit their skills against the batsmen, so they must also study the batsmen's weaknesses. The game is always a battle of wits: a battle between bat and ball to get the upper hand. Even the fastest bowlers constantly refine their techniques, and this allows the best of them, like Dennis Lillee, Richard Hadlee and Andy Roberts to name but three, to go on bowling with great success long after critics might have thought they should be thinking of retirement.

Bowling can be divided into four operations: the run-up, the leap into the delivery stride, the delivery itself and the follow-through.

The Run-up

The length of the run-up should be to suit yourself – obviously a slow bowler doesn't need as long a run-up as a fast bowler. A common fault is to take too long a run. I find 15 or 16 paces is ideal for me. You don't want to wear yourself out running all day. Work out how many paces you need so that you can arrive at the wicket with the momentum needed to bowl at the pace you require.

When practising, put down a marker from where you begin your run, and adjust it as practice continues until you have your marker in exactly the place you want it. Then starting at the bowling crease measure out the distance to your marker in easy paces. Once you know the length of your run-up in paces you can mark it out every time

1 Batsman's eye view of my delivery: I start my run, eyes on the batsman, head still, having gripped the ball in the way I intend to deliver.

2 I come in on a straight line smoothly increasing my speed as I go.

you come on to bowl in a match, knowing you will arrive at the bowling crease in the correct stride.

The essence of the run-up is balance. For a fast bowler like me, the run-up is designed to get me into the delivery stride perfectly balanced and at optimum speed, so everything should be as smooth as possible – no hops, jumps or little quirks.

I watched Martin Bicknell bowling for England in the Tests of 1993 and thought his run-up too long – he actually slowed up as he neared the wicket.

I find keeping the head still is essential, so watch the batsman all the way in. If you saw the head-on view of Linford Christie winning his 100 metres gold medal at the Olympic Games you will have noticed even at his speed how still his head was as he concentrated on

Marshall Law

■ Measure out your run-up carefully.
■ When running in, keep your head as still as possible, concentrating on smoothness and balance, and stay relaxed.
■ Build up your speed gradually, so that it is at its maximum as you approach the delivery stride.

the line. I try to keep mine as still. And like Linford I run in a straight line, and would advise anybody who wants to bowl fast to do the same. A curving run can only upset the

smoothness of it. I do not suggest that there has never been a good bowler with a curved run – I only relate my personal experiences and preferences!

3

My stride lengthens as I approach the bowling crease, the last two or three being at full stretch.

4

Just prior to the delivery leap ... I am at optimum speed, concentrating totally, head still and eyes on the spot where I intend the ball to pitch.

The Delivery Leap

SPEED should build up as you approach the bowling crease, and your stride will be at its widest. Assuming you are a right-hander, you leap into your delivery stride from the left foot, so that the right foot lands just behind the bowling crease in order for your left foot to cut the batting crease. This ensures that when you deliver the ball you are as close to the batsman as possible.

When you are running in your chest is facing the batsman but, as you bowl, you become more 'sideways on' as your left leg reaches down the pitch. I believe good fast bowling comes from strong abdominal muscles. The act of bowling pulls the torso round as the right arm comes over, and I believe a lot of back problems stem from needlessly overdoing this wrenching around of the body.

Therefore, so far as fast bowling is concerned, I disagree with those coaches who follow the MCC coaching book which advocates the right foot being parallel to the bowling crease. If you study the pictures on these and the next two pages of my back foot in the delivery stride you will notice it is pointing down the pitch.

The idea of having the back foot parallel to the bowling crease is to make sure the action is sideways on to the batsman. This is fine for swing or spin bowlers and I find it helps my own swing to plant the back foot more parallel to the crease.

Kapil Dev and Roger Binny are medium-fast bowlers who employ this copybook delivery. I used to

1 Just prior to planting my left foot my right arm comes up and begins to cock, ready to deliver the ball.

2 As I plant my left foot I am looking over my left shoulder at where the ball will pitch.

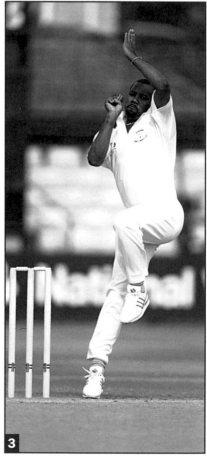

3 Note how my right foot is pointing down the wicket, saving strain on my back as I bring my arm over.

when young and hurt my back. I think this method can cause stress fractures. Most West Indians bowl with both feet pointing more or less forwards.

You will see that my front foot comes down in front of my back foot but the angle of my back foot gives me a slightly more 'open' look as I bring my right arm over. I believe it also saves me a lot of strain on my once-suspect back.

Make sure your left leg does not go across your right leg in the delivery stride (i.e. your left leg is more to the off side), otherwise you will be wrenching your body round even further.

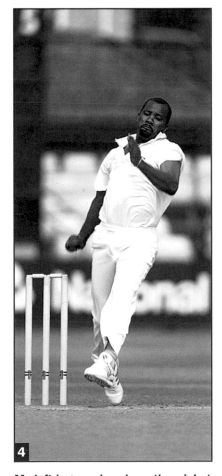

My left leg reaches down the wicket as my right arm begins to come over to bowl.

In mid-delivery stride bowling for the West Indies in the Prudential World Cup in England in 1983. This was the third World Cup, and the first that West Indies failed to win.

The Delivery

BOWLING is a fairly natural action, and I think that to describe it too carefully, part by part, only adds useless complications which puts the young bowler off. It's like analysing how you walk – if you think too hard about how you do it, you fall over!

Basically, as your right foot hits the ground, your body is leaning backward slightly (away from the batsman), with your left knee bent and raised high. As the left foot stretches forward, your left arm is high, and your right arm begins the delivery swing. As the left foot hits the pitch, your left arm is coming down and your right arm is swinging up behind you. When the ball reaches the top of the swing, the weight is on the left leg, with the body moving over it, the head in advance of the left foot, and the right foot having left the ground. This is when the ball is released. The left arm cuts away and the body turns to the left as the right arm comes down across the body and the right leg moves forward down the pitch.

Throughout the delivery keep the head steady and upright, with eyes fixed on the spot where you intend the ball to pitch.

The Follow-Through

The follow-through is not an afterthought. It is vital, especially if you are a fast bowler. You would injure your back if you pulled up dead, so you need a controlled, natural stop. Some fast bowlers feel the need to follow-through almost all the way down the pitch, but half-way should be sufficient for most bowlers. You mustn't straighten up too quickly or stop too quickly.

You will have been watching the pitch where you intend the ball to bounce, and as you follow through your eyes will pick up the flight of the ball.

1 The ball is released. My head has remained as still as possible all the time.

2 The ball is on the way, seam up. Just before the ball pitches I will pick up its flight.

You must be alert enough to do any fielding necessary, so you must follow the flight of the ball until it is safely fielded. Your other obligation is to run off the pitch as soon as possible. If you don't your feet will damage the pitch for the batsmen of both sides, and the umpire will warn you, and can ultimately ban you from bowling. There is an imaginary strip two feet (61 cm) wide down the centre of the pitch and starting four feet (1.22 m) in front of each popping crease which is sacred territory and on which you should never encroach. I usually bowl from close to the stumps and my follow through is almost straight, and I had one or two problems at first with the four-foot marker.

Marshall Law

■ Practise all aspects of the action. Remember if you are in the wrong position at the start of your delivery stride, you will be unable to correct the fault as you bowl.
■ Smoothness and timing bring power in bowling just as in batting, so do not sacrifice your action in an attempt to put more 'muscle' into it.
■ Regard the follow-through as your friend that eases your body back to relaxation after the explosive act of bowling.

3 I am still concentrating on the ball, ready to react to the batsman's shot in case I have to field the ball.

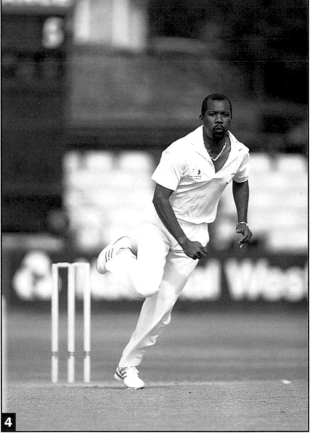

4 The ball has pitched and I continue to follow through. You can see I am beginning to move to the off side.

The Marshall Action Side-on View

THE sequence of photographs across the bottom of these two pages show my action from a side-on view.

It begins with the leap into the delivery stride, after I have made a smooth run to the crease, increasing my speed and length of stride as I come in. You can see from the first picture, where both my feet are off the ground, that my final leap is a long one. The back foot, with the toes pointing towards the batsman, has landed just before the bowling crease, so that when the outstretched left leg comes down the front foot cuts the popping crease.

Notice that in the delivery leap I am looking at where the ball will pitch from over my left shoulder. I keep my head as still as possible throughout the action, and release the ball when my right hand is at its height, giving the ball extra zip with my wrist movement.

The Grip

How do you grip the ball? This depends on the type of bowler you are, and as I am regarded as quite quick, I will deal here with the fast bowler's grip. Other grips will be discussed at the appropriate places later on.

The ball should always be gripped by the fingers, not by the palm of the hand. I hold the ball with the first two fingers close together on the seam, as illustrated in photograph 1, the thumb supporting the ball at the bottom, the third and fourth fingers cushioning the ball. The ball is held with the seam facing the batsman. This allows the seam to hit the pitch and produces movement off the pitch (see photographs 2 and 3 in the sequence on the previous page, where you can see the ball on its way seam up).

At the point of releasing the ball, I get extra 'zip' on the delivery by snapping the wrist forward (see photograph 2).

If the ball is swinging about too

1 I have leapt into my delivery stride. I do not jump too high, I concentrate on smoothness.

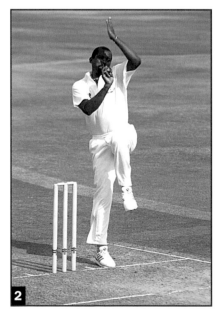

2 Back foot down, pointing down pitch; left knee bent and raised, left arm up; right arm raised ready for swing.

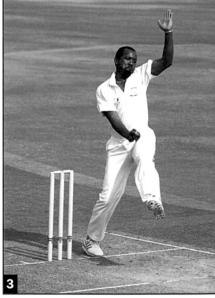

3 Right arm beginning its swing; left arm high; head still steady and watching point where ball will pitch.

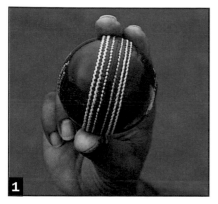

My normal grip for bowling fast.

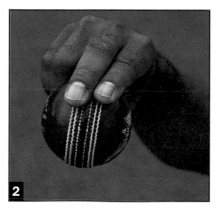

I use my wrist to help propel the ball.

Marshall Law

■ Practise all aspects of the action. Remember if you are in the wrong position at the start of your delivery stride, you will be unable to correct the fault as you bowl.

■ Smoothness and timing bring power in bowling just as in batting, so do not sacrifice your action in an attempt to put more 'muscle' into it.

■ Regard the follow-through as your friend that eases your body back to relaxation after the explosive act of bowling fast.

much and you don't want the ball to move off the seam, you can grip the ball across the seam (see the two photographs on page 20). This grip will ensure that the seam does not hit the pitch, and reduce swing.

Other grips for bowling inswing and outswing are illustrated on page 26, and those for off-cutters and leg-cutters are on page 28.

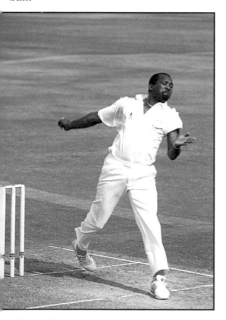

The left arm has come down as the right arm continues its swing, head still steady. Note I am reasonably 'sideways on' to the batsman.

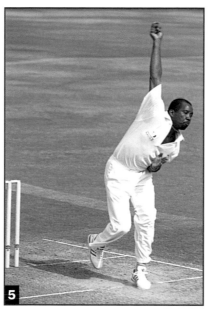

Weight on front foot; head in front of foot; right arm at its height about to release ball.

The ball delivered; I am following through.

Length and Line for Fast Bowling

The grip for a flat-side bouncer, which is also the grip to use when the ball is swinging too much.

The grip with the wrist snapped forward.

How often do you hear commentators and coaches talking of 'length and line'? These are the two cardinal virtues that a bowler can bring to his craft. If you can bowl to the length and line you want, you can keep batsmen quiet and go a long way to getting them out.

A Good Length

A good length ball is one which has the batsman in two minds. He doesn't know whether to play forward or back.

A good length ball for me is one that pitches three-quarters of the way down the pitch (see photograph below). It is difficult to drive and immediately puts doubt in the batsman's mind. He will usually stay rooted in his crease or play back – in either case he will have a ball at a difficult height to deal with.

You will know you are bowling a good length by where the batsman plays the ball. If you are bowling fast with a packed slip cordon looking to get an edge from the batsman, and he is comfortably playing you to mid-off, then your length is wrong. Don't be afraid to talk to the captain and discuss the matter if you suspect your length is not giving the batsman the trouble you expected.

Know the Batsman

I vary my length according to the batsman. Any top-class bowler knows the strengths, weaknesses, preferences and habits of the batsmen he is likely to bowl against. A good length ball, to a batsman who has a preference to play back, is one bowled further up to the bat than my usual length. Since the batsman is unlikely to come forward this gives the ball more chance to swing.

Similarly, with a batsman who likes to get on the front foot and is anxious to drive whenever he can, I will bowl just short of three-quarter length. This frustrates him and forces him on to the back foot, where he is less happy.

The Pitch and the Ball

The pitch could affect your length. On a fast, bouncy pitch, you could keep the ball up to try to bring the batsman forward. The batsman will be wanting to get on the back foot and digging the ball in short will probably be wasting a delivery. Similarly, if the pitch is slow and the batsman expecting to get forward, you should pitch it a little short.

At Southampton, where I had the pleasure to bowl for Hampshire from 1979 to 1993, one end of the square was much harder and bouncier than the other, so I had plenty to take into account when bowling there!

If the ball is new, keep it well up so that the batsman is brought forward. If the ball swings, you could get the outside edge; if it doesn't you might bowl him or get him lbw. If the ball is old, bowling a little short of a length is better.

The three-quarter length, 'good length' ball for a fast bowler. The batsman cannot decide quickly whether to go forward or back.

Headingley 1984. I've let rip a bouncer at Chris Broad who looks uncomfortable – an encouraging sight for a quickie.

Line

The fast bowler's line is somewhere in the area of off stump and just outside off stump. You are aiming for catches in the slip cordon.

If the ball is swinging away you might switch your line further to the leg, say middle and leg stump if the ball is really swinging. If the ball is swinging in a lot, then you will switch your line further to the off.

If you are bowling the Yorker, of course, then your line is straight at the stumps, down at the batsman's feet, and if you are bowling the bouncer, again the line is more towards the batsman, as your purpose is to shake up his confidence a little.

The Bouncer

Fast bowlers should be aggressive. A little psychological warfare is in order. Stare the batsman in the eye. My experience is that some look away, whereupon I feel I've won the battle. Some batsmen stare back. Good for them – it makes me more determined.

The bouncer is most effective if it is used as a surprise. If a batsman doesn't get on the front foot a lot you can safely pitch a few up to sweeten him and then let a surprise bouncer go to unsettle him.

The bouncer should pitch half-way down the pitch (see photograph below). It lifts awkwardly towards the batsman's head or chest and invites him to make a hurried or rash stroke. Bowl from wider on the crease so the ball will move in to the batsman.

On a hard wicket where the ball might bounce too high for the bouncer to be effective, you can try the flat side bouncer. This involves gripping the ball across the seam (see photographs opposite) so that the seam doesn't hit the pitch. Andy Roberts taught me this technique which makes the ball skid more – it doesn't fly so high.

This grip is also useful when the ball is swinging too much. By not allowing the seam to hit the pitch, you limit the ball's capacity to swing.

Even against players who play bouncers well – during my career, for example, Viv Richards and Ian Chappell were two of the best – it is always a tactic worth trying, if not overdone.

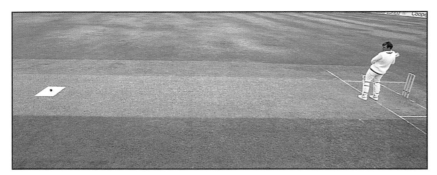

The length for a bouncer. The ball should reach the batsman around head high, at best inviting a rash stroke, at worst unnerving him.

Other Fast Bowling Weapons

The yorker is a particularly effective weapon against tail-enders. Here Joel Garner makes a mess of Pat Pocock's stumps.

IN the discussion of the bouncer on the previous page, mention was made of the yorker, which is almost the opposite of the bouncer. The yorker is the ball aimed to bounce on the popping crease, so that it squeezes under the bat as the batsman makes his downswing. It is almost as effective if aimed at the foot of the stumps – the result is often the same, as the batsman is too late getting his bat down.

Like the bouncer, the yorker should be bowled rarely, and used as a surprise weapon. It is best employed against a batsman who has been forced onto the back foot, especially if he is expecting a bouncer.

Nowadays it is impossible to bowl a string of bouncers to a batsman, because the Laws do not allow it, but it is legitimate to keep him on the back foot with a succession of short balls, and then to slip in the yorker. It works very well if it can be pitched somewhere near the batsman's toes, so that it is hitting leg stump. The batsman's rush to get his toes out of the way of both the ball and the bat as it comes down hard often leads to him missing the ball. And of course if he fails to get his toes out of the way he is still out lbw and with sore toes into the bargain.

The yorker can be used by bowlers of all speeds, and a swinging yorker can be very effective, but it is primarily the fast bowler's weapon. My West Indian colleagues Joel Garner and Patrick Patterson were particularly skilful with the yorker.

Change of Pace

Many fast bowlers bowl at their quickest all the time, but there are those who bowl within themselves. I am one of these, since I can bowl most effectively if I am not straining for that last extra foot of speed. As I've said before, smoothness and balance are more profitable than unco-ordinated exertion. But this gives me the chance of slipping in now and then a quicker ball. Such a change of pace can be very disconcerting for a batsman who has got into a steady groove. The yorker is a particularly good ball to

Franklyn Stephenson bowling for Notts in 1989. At that time his slower ball was a lethal weapon expertly delivered.

A correct position of the front foot. Even if my heel is raised, it is clearly behind the back edge of the marking.

bowl with that extra little bit of pace.

To most fast bowlers change of pace, however, means a slower one. Here the main element is disguise. The run-up action and the speed that the arm comes over must all be identical with what has gone before. This makes it difficult to bowl the ball slower – one way is to bowl a fast leg-break, which is slower than the normal delivery without slowing down the arm action.

If the batsman is fooled, he plays too early at the ball, and the bowler must be ready for a caught and bowled chance. A bowler who has exploited the slower bowl really well in recent years is Franklyn Stephenson, who did the 'double' in 1988 for Notts. However it was noticeable that in that extraordinary NatWest final in 1993, when Warwickshire scored 322 to win, Franklyn, who was bowling for Sussex, seemed temporarily to have lost the knack. It is a very difficult

art to perfect, but it is a valuable weapon in any bowler's armoury, especially a fast bowler's.

No-balling

Too many bowlers give away too many runs with no-balls. I can hear you say the West Indies haven't been too good on keeping the extras down in the past, and I agree. But it is still very bad cricket, and every bowler should at least know where his feet

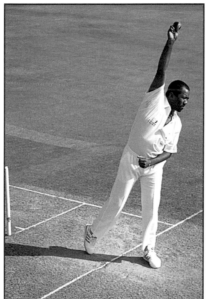

No ball! The front foot is beyond the popping crease.

must be to deliver a fair bowl.

The front foot is allowed to cut the popping crease. The actual crease is the back edge of the line marking the crease (i.e. the edge nearer the stumps) and provided a part of the foot, either grounded or raised, is behind this line, the delivery is a fair one.

The back foot must be within the return crease, which is the inside edge of the marking at right-angles to the bowling crease. In this case the whole foot must be within, and not touching this crease.

Marshall Law

■ Use the yorker as a surprise weapon. If the batsman has just hit you for four, he might expect a bouncer. York him!
■ Practise your slower ball in the nets. Remember: anybody can bowl slow – what you are trying to do is bowl slow while making it look fast.

In both cases, the creases are regarded as of infinite length, and don't stop where the marking stops.

I scratch a little mark behind the bowling crease further back than I actually need it as a guide for my back foot. I know if my back foot lands around this mark my front foot will be OK, and I have a little margin for error.

No ball! My back foot is outside the return crease. Even if it were only touching the inside edge of the marking it would be a no-ball.

Using the Crease

THE initiative always lies with the bowler in cricket. It is he who gets the action started, and he who dictates what is going to happen. The batsman, by contrast, can only react to what the bowler delivers. So one of the bowler's aims is to keep the batsman guessing, and one way to do this is to vary the line of attack.

By changing the spot from where you bowl, you can pose the batsman slightly different problems with each ball. All types of bowlers use this tactic, although on the whole slow bowlers will practise it more than quick bowlers.

As I have mentioned earlier, rhythm and balance are essential to a fast bowler and I like getting my action smoothly grooved. But the bowlers I learned most from – Andy Roberts, who thought deeply about cricket, and Joel Garner and Michael Holding, who were always ready to help a newcomer – taught me the value of variety: never bowl two successive balls alike, they said. An important variation lies in the use of the crease.

On the whole I run in straight and bowl from as close to the stumps as possible. You can see from the photograph how close my back foot and right hand are to the wicket.

The reason for bowling close to the stumps is to give yourself a much better chance of getting an lbw decision. Umpires will not give a batsman out lbw unless they can see clearly that the ball would have hit the wicket. If they can see the ball is travelling and pitching in a straight line between the wickets, they might rule in your favour, but if the ball is angling in, then they must have doubts.

In the second photograph I am not using the whole width of the bowling crease, but you can see I am bowling from some two feet (around 60 cm) wider. This unsettles the batsman, as the ball is on a slightly different line. And don't forget his bat is only $4\frac{1}{4}$ inches (10.8 cm) wide, and if you can hit the edge of it you can get him out.

It is a good tactic for a fast bowler to bowl the bouncer from wide of the stumps. This has the effect of spearing the ball in towards the batsman, and makes it harder for him to leave alone.

For the same reason swing bowlers will use the width of the crease to get the right direction of the ball at the batsman's end. If you bowl outswing, for instance, and the ball is swinging a lot, allowing the batsman to let the ball pass harmlessly wide of the wicket, you can bowl from the edge of the crease. The initial direction of the ball will be coming in to the batsman, and the outswing will take the ball much closer to the off stump than before.

For slow bowlers, variety is even more important than for quick bowlers. They will use the width of the crease as much as possible to vary their line and flight.

Bowling from behind the Crease

Again, bowling from behind the crease is a tactic more used by slow bowlers, particularly off-spin bowlers, than it is by fast bowlers, who want to deliver the ball from as close to the batsman as possible. But it's not a bad idea for a fast bowler occasionally to slip in a delivery from a yard or so farther back. This has a similar effect to delivering the slower ball,

Bowling from close to the stumps gives you the best chance of getting an lbw decision.

Bowling from wide of the stumps spears the ball in towards the batsman, causing him problems.

1

I am bowling round the wicket using the full width of the crease. My back foot is landing just inside the return crease.

2

The delivery stride. The action is the same (see photo on page 15) but the ball is delivered at a very different angle.

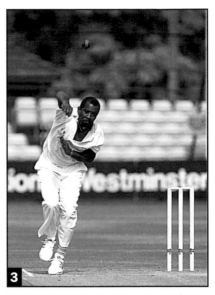

3

The ball is delivered (seam up) from four feet (1.2 m) wide of the stumps. The follow-through is to my right.

but don't forget that at my speed the batsman still has only about half a second to react – not much time to think about what to do!

Round the Wicket

Going round the wicket is another tactic used more by slow bowlers. The off-spinner, for instance, straightens the ball to a right-hander by bowling from round the wicket, with the consequent better chance of lbw. Inswing bowlers might go round the wicket for the same reason.

If you decide to bowl round the wicket, of course, you must notify the umpire who informs the batsman and gives him a fresh guard if required, so the surprise element is removed.

However it still has the same unsettling effect. I often bowl round the wicket in the Caribbean where batsmen get used to bowling coming from over the wicket and on the hard wickets they quickly get themselves into a groove. The variation of angle forces them to

think about the line and make adjustments to their positioning.

In England I will often bowl round the wicket to left-handers, and like to use as much of the crease as I can (see photographs). The left-hander will expect the ball to be coming in to him all the time. If it starts on the off stump he is going to play on the leg side, and if the ball straightens it is a good ball. It might get him leg-before, caught in the

slips, or caught off a leading edge.

Be careful when going round the wicket. I find this is when I have most problems with no-balls as the stride pattern is not quite the same. Also it is more difficult to run off the wicket as you follow through, because you must go in the opposite direction to normal. If you run across the pitch the umpire will warn you. Practise the follow-through in the nets.

Marshall Law

■ Use the crease to keep the batsman guessing. If nothing much is happening, a change of bowling position might provoke an error.

■ Keep thinking about dismissing the batsman. If he's using his pads a lot think of what angle of delivery will put him in danger of being lbw.

Swinging the Ball

WHY the ball swings is known to science – why sometimes it swings more than others and how some bowlers get it to swing more than others is still a mystery – even to some of us bowlers!

Basically the ball swings because one side is polished and the other is rough. The air flows more smoothly past the polished side, and becomes turbulent on the rough side. The seam forms part of the rough side. The differing air flow exerts different pressures on the ball, causing it to swing in the direction of the rough side.

When the ball is new, both sides are shiny of course, but the position of the seam gives the necessary roughness to one side.

Bowlers of all speeds can swing the ball, but the slower the delivery the more chance the difference in air pressure has to work. For this reason it was thought at one time that swing was a specialist skill of the medium

pacers. Indeed it is, but not of the medium-pacer only. I think I can claim to be one of those bowlers who, in the 1980s, proved that the very fastest can make the ball swing.

Fast bowlers, of course, were thought to be speed merchants only. So why does anybody bother to bowl medium-pace if the ball can swing and cut almost as much for a fast bowler? The answer is accuracy.

It is no good being able to make the ball swing if you cannot control the length and direction. It was the deadly accuracy of Derek Shackleton of Hampshire which captured so many wickets for him over the years. He took 100 wickets in 20 consecutive seasons, a world record.

I have given an Englishman as an example because English conditions are often ideal for swing bowling – humid conditions with low cloud cover. The Pakistani Waqar Younis did some remarkable things in England in 1992.

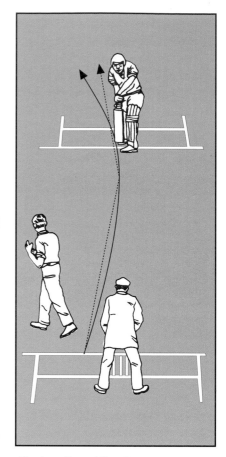

The length and line for an outswinger. The object is to find the outside edge. The dotted line shows the leg-cutter (see page 28), for which the principles are similar.

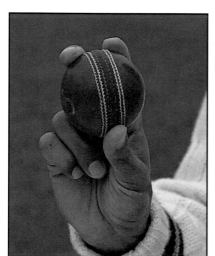

The grip for the outswinger, the seam pointing towards first slip.

The grip for the inswinger. The seam points towards fine leg.

The Outswinger

The outswinger is lethal, and probably gets as many wickets as any delivery in cricket. You alter your grip slightly so that the seam is pointing towards the slips – first slip, say (see photograph). The rough side of the ball is to the left (I assume a right-handed batsman and bowler in these descriptions).

However, I advise you to experiment with the grip. Some players hold the ball slightly differently, some can make the ball swing later by pointing the seam

The length and line for an inswinger. The object is to find the gap between bat and pad or the inside edge for a bat-pad catch to short leg. The dotted line shows the off-cutter (see next spread), for which the principles are similar.

Marshall Law

■ Don't forget accuracy is essential for swing bowling. It is sometimes worth sacrificing speed for accuracy, but not the other way round.

■ Remember the grip shown in the photograph on page 21, for the flat-sided bouncer. This will be useful if the ball is swinging uncontrollably and you find you are bowling so wide you are giving away wides.

■ Experiment with your own grips for swinging the ball. You might beat us all at it.

batsman less time to adjust, encouraging him to 'feel' for the ball and perhaps to snick it to the slips.

The Inswinger

The inswinger is the opposite ball to the outswinger. The ball is held with the seam pointing towards fine leg, with the shiny side this time on the left (see photograph). Some bowlers use a more open-chested action, but it is not necessary provided the wrist is behind the ball pushing the seam in the desired direction.

The ball is pitched up as for the outswinger, but the line is more to the off, on or outside off stump (see diagram left). The idea is to find the gap between bat and pad, or to get an lbw or an inside edge. A misdirected ball on middle or leg stump could be expensive, as it might be helped down to the fine-leg boundary.

closer to the batsman. Don't be afraid to experiment.

As the ball is released the wrist is kept stiff and the fingers push the ball with the hand behind the ball. The ball should be delivered from close to the stumps, although if the ball is swinging a lot, you can move further out.

The line should be around middle and off stump to make batsmen play, and the length should be as far up as possible (see diagram above). This gives the ball the maximum opportunity to swing and gives the

Waqar Younis swung the ball to great effect in 1992 against England. Here Graham Gooch has just been bowled in the Trent Bridge one-day game.

Bowling Cutters

THE off-cutter and the leg-cutter are, like swing bowling, weapons mainly of the medium-pacer, although there is no reason why fast bowlers should not bowl them, and indeed Dennis Lillee, undoubtedly fast and a fast bowler I admired almost more than any other, would often bowl effective cutters. The most famous cutter of the ball, though, is probably Alec Bedser of Surrey and England, who was fast-medium.

The Off-cutter

The effect of the off-cutter is really that of a fast off-break. The ball is gripped with the first two fingers fairly close together above the seam and the thumb gripping the seam and supporting the ball from below, the inside of the thumb pressing into the seam (see photograph).

This is my grip, but here again I suggest you find what is most comfortable and what works best for you. Most bowlers hold the ball with the fingers along the seam rather than across it as in my method. They would point the seam at the batsman, or towards fine leg as for the inswinger, whereas in my grip the seam points more to the leg-side.

At the height of the delivery, when the ball is released, you cut your first finger down the outside of the ball quite sharply to impart spin while the hand rotates in a clockwise direction.

This wrist action adds zip to the

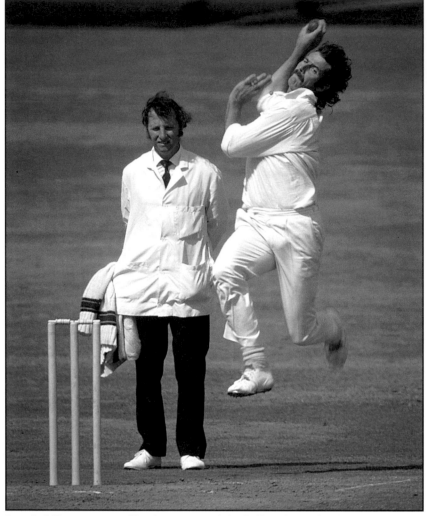

Dennis Lillee – a very effective cutter of the ball and very fast!

The grip for the off-cutter. In delivery spin is imparted by cutting the fingers down the outside of the ball.

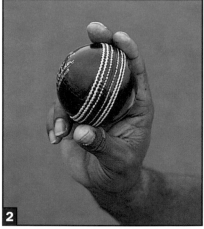

The grip for the leg-cutter. In delivery spin is imparted by cutting the fingers down the inside of the ball.

finger action and the ball cuts off the pitch towards the leg side. It is a good ball for the outswing bowler to perfect, as the batsman gets used to the ball swinging away and suddenly finds one cutting in the other way, and hopefully gets bowled between bat and pad.

The off-cutter's line is just outside off-stump and well pitched up, so that it cuts in late towards the batsman's legs (see diagram, page 27). If he plays for the ball which comes straight on he could get a nick onto his pad and be caught at short leg.

The Leg-cutter

The leg-cutter is a devastating ball which resembles a fast leg-break. A good one is likely to get even top batsmen out.

Here again the grips employed by top bowlers and coaches vary. Mine, as shown in the photograph, has the first two fingers close together and across the seam at an angle. The thumb is opposite, gripping the seam, and the middle finger is helping to keep the ball steady. Some bowlers prefer to have the fingers further apart and running more along the seam than across it. You should find what is best for you.

At the point of delivery this time, the fingers are pulled down the inside of the ball, spinning it in an anti-clockwise direction.

It is an awkward movement which is again assisted by the wrist, and only comes from long practice.

As with all swingers and cutters, the ball should be well pitched up and be pitched on middle or middle and off stumps (see diagram, page 26). It is a useful ball for the predominantly in swing bowler, as the ball will move the other way. You'll be looking for catches in the slips.

Marshall Law

■ Speed can get wickets on its own, but the bowler who can cut the ball has a valuable additional weapon in his armoury.
■ The cutter is an attacking ball. Think positively and aim to get the batsman out with it.

Alec Bedser of Surrey and England (pictured with twin brother Eric) took 236 Test wickets with his fast-medium deliveries, many of them cutters.

Fieldsetting for Swing Bowlers

IT IS no good being a great bowler and encouraging the batsman to mistime and snick the ball here, there and everywhere if the fielders aren't in the correct places to make the catches.

So far as fast bowling is concerned, I have been lucky to be a part of the greatest fast bowling attack in history. With all due respect to Wes Hall, the great West Indian bowler of the early 1960s, the supremacy en masse of West Indian fast bowling began in the mid-1970s with Andy Roberts, and since then Joel Garner, Colin Croft, Michael Holding, myself, Curtly Ambrose and others have kept West Indies fast bowling at the top of the tree.

But I don't think we've ever used a field quite so attacking as the famous Carmody 'Umbrella' field, invented by Keith Carmody, the captain of the Australian Services team in England at the end of the Second World War. With Keith Miller to bowl, he used only a token mid-off in front of the wicket with everybody else in an umbrella from short leg to gully to hold on to the snicks.

Outswing Bowling

There is no need to be as extreme as this. Let us consider first an attacking field I might set if I were bowling outswing and getting something from the wicket.

I will need at least three slips and a gully to hold the catches since the area from wicket-keeper to gully is where I am hoping to get the wickets. If I am defending a big total where giving away an occasional boundary is not critical, I might well have another slip, but let us assume discretion here and use this player at third man to save boundaries accruing from those snicks which will inevitably speed through the slips without going to hand. I might have a short leg to hold the catches from a batsman fending off a bouncer, and a long leg to catch out those batsmen who connect with a bouncer but not well enough to clear the boundary. A mid-off and a mid-on will chase everything which the batsman manages to hit in front of the wicket – thereby saving my legs (see diagram 1).

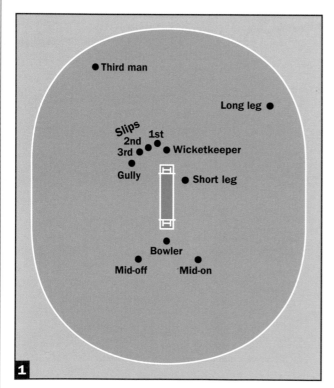

1

An attacking field for an outswing bowler.

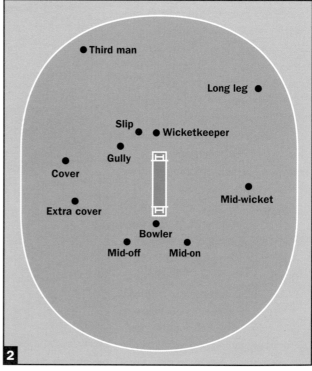

2

A defensive field for an outswing bowler.

If later on the contest gets more even, or if the wicket is a featherbed, the slip field will get denuded and two will move to cover and extra cover to stop those squarish drives and the short leg might move to mid-wicket (diagram 2). These fields might also suffice for the leg-cutter.

Inswing Bowling

If I were bowling inswing on a helpful wicket I would still need a slip presence, but will need more emphasis on the leg-side field. Two slips and a gully might suffice on the off-side, but only two men are allowed to be behind the wicket on the leg side. I would usually have a long leg for the hook and a short fine leg (or leg slip). I would also have two short legs, square and slightly forward, and a mid-wicket. A mid-off or a cover point to parade the off-side area in front of the wicket would give me a

reasonably attacking field (see diagram 3). If the batsmen were completely defensive I might even attack further by bringing my long leg up to reinforce the leg-side cordon of close catchers.

If the circumstances of the match demanded a more defensive field, one of the slips could go to third man or short third man and the gully could go deeper and squarer to cover point, while the leg slip might move across to extra cover. The short square leg would then move deeper to a more conventional square leg position, while the forward short leg would go to mid-on, mid-wicket moving a little squarer (see diagram 4). A bowler who employs off-cutters would use fields like those described for an inswing bowler, but not, of course, if the off-cutter is used only as a variation on outswing. Most of these players will be in a position to save the single.

Marshall Law

■ Don't feel inhibited by the fact that certain fielding positions have been dignified with a name. You are entitled to place your men where you like (within the laws and the restrictions of the competition).
■ Don't be slow to change your field if you spot a weakness in the batsman or if the ball begins to behave unexpectedly. Don't make a show of it – discuss your idea quietly with the captain.
■ Having set your field, bowl to it. Think of yourself and the fielders as a single unit, working to contain and dismiss the batsman.

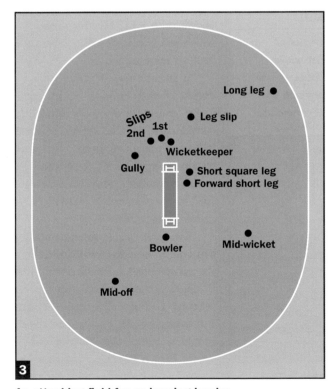

3

An attacking field for an inswing bowler.

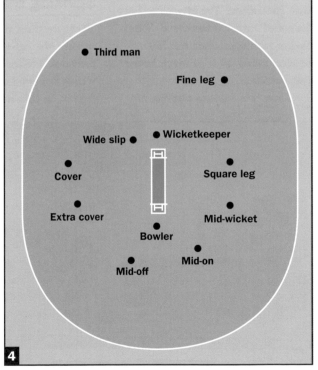

4

A defensive field for an inswing bowler.

Spin Bowling

THERE has been a great revival recently in top-class cricket of spin bowling, particularly leg-spin bowling. After years when some critics seriously thought that the nature of cricket was changing and that spin bowlers were museum items from the past, along comes Shane Warne to have enough success in the early 1990s to make spinners fashionable again.

Of course the West Indies, the islands of Ramadhin and Valentine and Lance Gibbs, were mainly responsible for this because we built up such a battery of fast bowlers from the 1970s onwards that we became invincible – we could win with pace alone. The idea of a 'balanced' attack disappeared. Why bother with spin when the fast bowlers could do it all much better and quicker.

There were always pockets of resistance. In India and Pakistan the spin bowling tradition was harder to change, and some great leg-break bowlers like Abdul Qadir and Mushtaq Ahmed continued to have success at every level. Most English counties had a spinner, and they remained valuable in county cricket, but none of them really shone consistently at Test level.

Shane Warne came into international prominence in the Second Test against West Indies in Australia in 1992–93, picking up seven for 52 in the second innings as Australia won the match. His team mate, off-spinner Tim May, took five for 9 in the fourth Test, and even though it was the bowling of Curtly Ambrose that had the last word in the series, the spinners looked as if they were back. The way Warne bamboozled the English batsmen in the summer of 1993 made everybody sit up and take notice.

Spinning the Ball

There are three main types of spinner, the off-spinner and the orthodox left-arm spinner, whose spin is imparted mainly with the fingers, so that these bowlers are usually called finger-spinners, and the leg-break and googly bowler, who imparts much more of the spin with the wrist, so he is usually classified as a wrist-spinner.

Spin bowlers are the improvisers of cricket – they have their own styles and methods. Anybody who wishes to be a spinner must experiment for himself, trying out all sorts of spin and methods of achieving it before deciding on what is best for him.

Work and Practice

Once a player has discovered a knack for spinning the ball and has the ambition to go further, it is a question of practice and practice. He can also strengthen his fingers and wrists. The keeping of a rubber ball as a constant companion when travelling or walking, for example, will help, for the constant squeezing of it will help strengthen the fingers. It is not a bad idea to practise bowling initially with a ball like this – one which will spin a lot and give you the 'feel' of spinning the ball.

At an early stage a player must decide whether to be an off-spinner or leg-spinner. It is impossible to combine the two and remain accurate in both. In any case, even if you were reasonably proficient at both you couldn't combine them in a bowling spell, as the field would need to be re-set for each change.

Find what you do most naturally, and concentrate on that. Generally the off-spinner has more control, and in English county cricket over the years has had easily the most success. But covered wickets have gone some way to removing this disparity, and on the harder, bouncier wickets to be found in Australia, the West Indies and Pakistan, for example, the leg-

Lance Gibbs, the West Indian off-spinner, who took 309 wickets in Test cricket, at the time the world record.

spinner has proved more effective.

Certainly a top-class leg-spinner can cause havoc among the best sides, and I suspect that if the success of Warne, in particular, continues, then there will be lots of young cricketers taking up leg-spin in the next few years.

Concentrate on the Spin

Although all bowling is useless if the length and line of the delivery cannot be controlled, and this is particularly true of spin bowling, I suggest that initially the budding spinner concentrates on just that: being a spinner.

You often hear cricket commentaries where a slow bowler is on and the commentator is saying that the ball isn't turning, and we've all heard of the famous slow bowlers

Marshall Law

■ First of all experiment to decide what sort of spin suits you.
■ Strengthen your fingers and wrists so that you can spin the ball without getting tired quickly.
■ Think spin, spin, spin. Worry about flight and length and line only when you know you're a spinner.

who could hardly turn the ball but who had such mastery of flight, length and 'tactical cunning' that they could get their wickets without spinning much.

I say forget all that. Learn the niceties and the 'cunning' later. If you want to be a spinner the first thing to learn is how to spin the ball and make it turn. Concentrate on that.

Shane Warne takes Atherton's wicket with another fizzing leg-spinner during his first Test against England in 1993, where he took a wicket with his first ball and continued to dominate all summer.

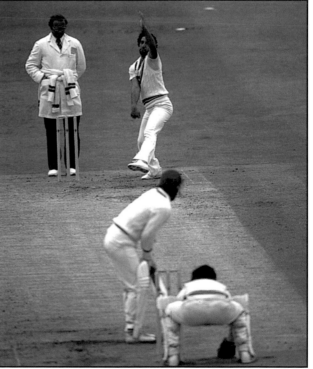

Another leg-spinning match-winner, Abdul Qadir of Pakistan, shields the ball in the back of his hand making his deliveries almost impossible to read. Like Warne, he could bowl googlies and top-spinners as well.

Bowling Off-Spin

OFF-SPIN bowlers are often regarded as 'stock' bowlers. This means that their accuracy (off-spinners must be accurate) allows them to bowl for long periods defensively. This is not to say that they cannot be attacking bowlers, but merely that a captain with a good off-spinner in his side knows that he has one bowler whom he can put on safely in almost any situation. In English county cricket, where conditions are held to suit off-spin, this has led to the off-spinner being the backbone of many a side. It has sometimes been thought that off-spinners would not flourish so well on the harder wickets abroad, but

Jim Laker, whose first Test series was in the West Indies, proved to be easily England's best bowler. And of course Lance Gibbs, the great West Indian off-spinner who once held the record number of Test wickets at 309, although he did pretty well in England, took more than two-thirds of these on hard wickets. Roger Harper and Carl Hooper are more recent West Indian off-spinners, who both come from Georgetown and developed their skills to Test standard in Guyana.

Off-spinners Grip

The ball is gripped by the forefinger and the second finger, both across the seam, with the top joints of these two fingers pressed firmly into the seam (photograph 1). These two fingers are the spinning fingers and are spaced well apart. But the size of people's hands vary, and people with smaller hands will find the thumb also gripping the ball, running along

the seam, and the third finger becoming part of the grip too. The ball must not be in the palm of the hand, however, but in the fingers, for it is the top joints of the spinning fingers which impart the spin, in particular the forefinger.

The ball is spun clockwise. Go through the motions of grasping a door knob with your fingers to open a door. As you turn it clockwise your wrist will turn towards you (photograph 2). Your palm will turn upwards. It is this wrist action, at the point of delivery, coupled with the fingers pulling along and down the seam, which sends the ball off spinning.

Off-spinner's Action

The smooth run-up is as essential for a slow bowler as a fast bowler, but of course it need not be so long or so fast. But it must be smooth and controlled, and the head should be as still as ever. The run-up for a slow

1 The grip for the off-spinner. A bowler with small hands will use the thumb to hold the ball too, but it will not play a part in imparting spin.

2 As the ball is delivered, the wrist turns from facing the on-side to the off, as the fingers are pulled down the seam, giving the ball an extra flick.

Tim May leaps into his delivery stride. His back foot lands well in front of the bowling crease, as his delivery stride is a very short one.

Note how sideways-on May is as he prepares to bowl. His left foot will cut the popping crease and he will swivel hard on it, bringing his body round as he bowls.

bowler is not just something to get him to the crease – in fact an off-spinner's bowling arm will come over quite fast and a co-ordinated action is essential.

A little hop into the delivery stride will get you sideways on and leaning back away from the batsman. The delivery stride should not be a long one, because you want to deliver the ball from as great a height as possible, bounce being a great ally of the off-spinner. Incidentally it helps if you are tall if you want to bowl off-spin – all those mentioned above are tall men.

The front foot should be planted slightly across the line of delivery i.e. further to the on-side than the back foot. This will enable you to use the front leg as a pivot and bring the body round hard. The bowling arm comes over late and across the body

with the fingers pulling down the side of the ball as it is released.

It is as important as ever to follow through. In fact, if you deliver the ball properly, you will almost be forced to follow through because you will have put a lot of energy into the delivery.

Marshall Law

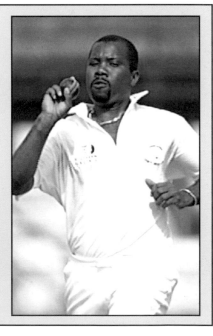

■ Always try to spin the ball as much as you can. A spinner who doesn't spin is like a tiger without teeth.

■ Think of your whole action, from run-up to follow-through, as designed to deliver a vicious spinner. Do not think of the actual moment of releasing the ball as the only thing that counts, or you will start bowling gentle lobs or half-volleys.

■ Keep your head still. Be smoooth!

Off-Spinners' Variations and Fields

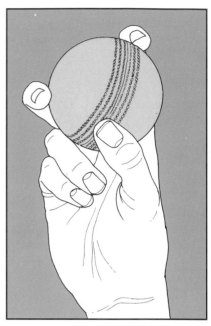

The grip for the arm-ball. If delivered from close to the stumps, or from around the wicket, it will go on towards the slips.

THE off-spinner has those variations which are open to all types of bowler: the use of the crease, the change of line, the slower ball, changes in flight, etc. Where these are common of all spinners they are discussed on pages 46-47. However, there are certain deliveries the off-spinner can mix in with his stock ball to keep the batsman on his toes and set him new problems.

It is often said that off-spinners in a long spell are 'nagging away', and tying the batsman down with their accuracy. This is fine, but if the off-spinner bowls the same delivery all the time, he is not going to get the batsman out. A batsman can be just as patient as the bowler, and he is not going to do anything rash – he will just wait for a ball he can hit to the boundary and then settle down to be 'nagged' at for another spell.

The arm-ball and the floater are two deliveries with which the off-spinner can keep the batsman on his toes.

The Arm-ball

The arm-ball is so-called because the ball 'goes on with the arm' instead of turning. The grip is the same as for the off-break, except that the seam is differently placed. Instead of the top joints of the first two fingers being across the seam, they are now each side of it, gripping the smooth surface of the ball (diagram 1).

The action is much the same as for the off-break but the fingers do not pull down the seam, but slide down the shiny side of the ball. Obviously less effort is put into this action, and into the wrist movement, because you don't want the ball to spin. But you put enough into it to lead the batsman to think it is a stock ball which is coming towards him. It should be a good length, so

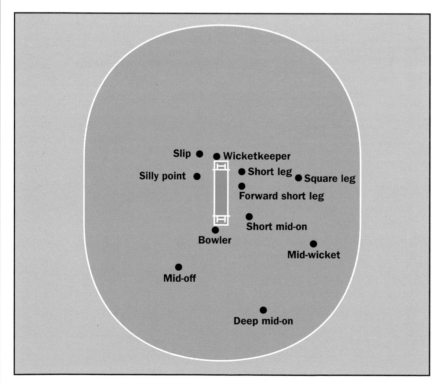

An attacking field for an off-spinner pitching around middle, middle and leg. Forward short leg could perhaps be moved to cover, with mid-wicket going squarer to compensate and cover the space.

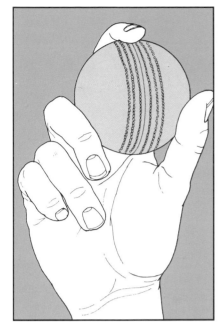

One grip for bowling the floater. The technique is like that for bowling an outswinger, and the effect is to drift the ball away to the off.

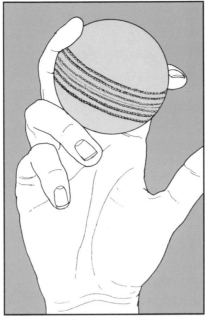

Alternative grip for bowling the floater. The position of the hand means the ball spins on a horizontal axis rather than a vertical one.

Marshall Law

■ Accuracy is fine, but don't become predictable. Think before every ball and try to surprise the batsman.
■ Vary the field according to the batsman. If he is prodding forward have close catchers both sides of the wicket, but if he is itching to drive keep two men posted on the fence behind you.

that if he plays for the break, and the ball goes straight on, he could get caught at slip.

Floater

This is very similar to the arm-ball. There are two ways of bowling it. In the first the ball is gripped with the first two fingers wide apart, the first finger running along the seam. The thumb and second finger form the other two points of a triangle holding the ball (diagram 2).

At the moment of delivery, the wrist is behind the ball and the seam vertical. You do not spin the ball or rotate the wrist but push the ball towards slip with the first finger. This is very similar to the method of bowling an outswinger and the object

is to get the ball to drift towards the slips. It is not an easy ball to disguise, because the action is unlike that of the off-break, but if it works can prove very useful.

The second method of bowling the floater is to grip the ball as for the standard off-break (diagram 3), but at the moment of delivery to turn the wrist so that the side of the hand faces the batsman rather than the front. The ball spins on a horizontal axis, like a top-spinner, rather than on a vertical axis, and instead of turning is more likely to drift away in the air towards slips.

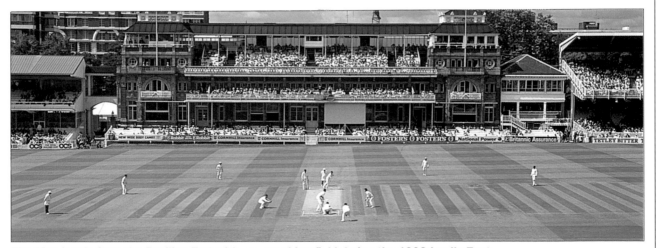

Tim May bowls from the Pavilion End with an attacking field during the 1993 Lord's Test.

Bowling Leg-Spin

little quirks and fancies in the run-up, a kangaroo leap here, a strange twist of the arm there, and some of them bowl as if they are going into contortions to produce a rabbit from a hat. So if you are an aspiring leg-spinner, do not worry if your method

effect. Do not add any frills just for show. They are almost bound to be counter-productive.

The Grip

The ball is held by the first three fingers, well spaced apart. The first

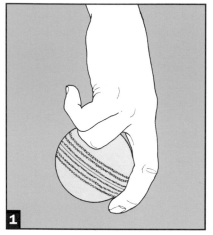

1

The leg-spinner's grip, the first two fingers spaced out across the seam.

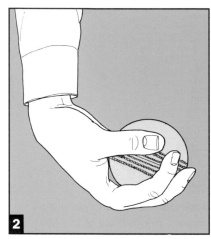

2

The grip from the other side, the thumb resting on the seam.

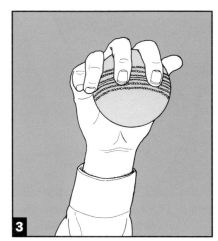

3

The wrist flips round in an anti-clockwise direction.

As I write this book, leg spin is enjoying a revival with Shane Warne producing a few fireworks. Leg-spinners are certainly fun to watch. It is a difficult art and occasionally goes wrong. Leg-spinners are either getting hit all over the place or bowling a batsman round his legs. In my last match at Southampton in 1993, a charity match against some old West Indian Test friends, I ended the match with an over of leg-breaks, not without success. It's exciting stuff to bowl or watch.

The value of a leg-spinner is that he can demoralise the opposition. Batsman who cannot read the googly, or who are beaten by several inches by misjudging the break, become edgy. They take risks and get out and before long the whole side seems to be at panic stations.

Leg-break bowlers are individualists. They have their own

is not copy book. On the other hand, remember the principle of the run-up – to deliver you at the bowling crease with a motion that allows you to bowl with maximum

two fingers lie across the seam with the top joints pressing into them. The third finger is bent so that the top joint lies parallel to the seam, at its edge. The base of the thumb rests

1

Shane Warne's delivery action. Umpire Dickie Bird checks that all's well as he makes a small jump into his delivery stride.

lightly on the seam. It is the helped by the third finger, which is going to impart the spin.

The grip is the same for all the leg spinner's classic deliveries: leg-break, googly and top-spinner. It is the action of the wrist at the moment of delivery which determines the spin.

The Leg-Break

The wrist is bent as the arm reaches the top of the delivery swing, and as the arm comes over the palm of the hand is facing the batsman. The wrist flips round in an anti-clockwise direction as the ball is released, with the third finger giving the ball an extra impetus, so that the ball leaves the hand spinning on a vertical axis anti-clockwise.

The Googly

The wrist rotates earlier than for the leg-break, so that when the ball is released the back of the hand is facing the batsman. this means the ball comes out of the hand over the top of the third and little fingers, and

the spin is reversed – the ball becomes an off-break.

The Top-Spinner

The flip of the wrist this time begins earlier than for the leg-break but later than for the googly, so that the spin is on a horizontal axis, and instead of the ball breaking to one side or the other it will hold its line and hurry on to the batsman.

All these variations are dependent upon fine timing, and in fact leg-break bowlers frequently mistime their wrist rotations and bowl a ball different to the one intended. It is this which makes them so unpredictable, and makes life very difficult of the batsman.

The Action

A good pivot on the front leg is necessary to reinforce the wrist action and add zip to the delivery. The delivery arm must be straight and locked at the elbow. The right arm should swing right across the body pulling the body right round on the left leg. The head should be as still as possible throughout.

ane Warne delivers the ball very side on, looking over ther than inside his left arm at where he will pitch the ball.

A vigorous anti-clockwise flick of the wrist dictates the enormous spin he puts on the ball.

Leg-Spinners' Variations and Fields

THE leg-spinner is an attacking bowler. No captain brings on a leg-spinner to keep the runs down. The leg-spinner is expected to do something spectacular. He is, above all, the bowler that makes things happen.

He should bowl most of the time from over the wicket, so that his leg-break straightens up to the right-hand batsman. From round the wicket the ball will go across the batsman, and anything pitched outside the leg stump the batsman can safely play with his pads, since he cannot be out lbw.

It is essential that he should keep the ball up, because anything short is likely to be severely punished. He mustn't give the batsman an opportunity to wait and see which way the ball will turn and by how much – he must commit him to a stroke.

The googly is one of the most exciting balls in cricket, but it should not be overdone. Keep it as a surprise and do not make it a stock ball. It is not a bad idea to try one fairly early on to a batsman who has just come in – he is unlikely to feel confident enough to spot it and punish it.

When bowling the googly you are expecting to fool the batsman into thinking the ball is a leg-break; there is no point in bowling it otherwise. Therefore bowl it so that it will hit the wicket – it's frustrating to beat the batsman if you don't get him out. You are merely giving him practice at spotting the next one. So pitch the googly on or just outside the off stump, so that it will hit the wicket if he 'lets it go harmlessly past'.

To soften up the batsman for this coup, you may need to feed him a few leg-breaks around the off-stump

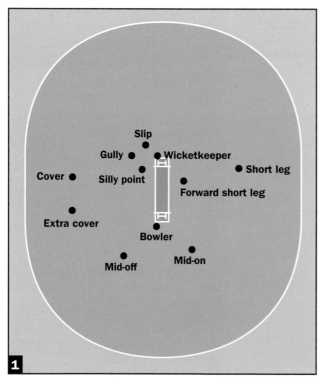

1

An attacking field for a leg-spinner. Some leg-spinners might want another man behind the stumps, perhaps dispensing with gully.

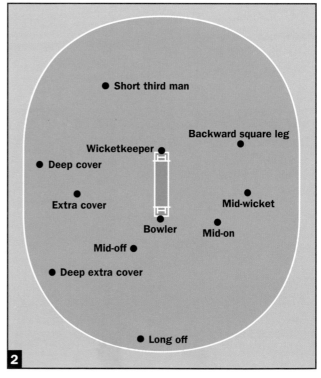

2

A field for a leg-spinner when the batsmen are hitting out and there is little for him in the wicket. He is hoping for catches sliced into the off-side field.

Shane Warne bowls to an attacking field during the fifth England v Australia Test at Edgbaston in 1993.

to get him used to the ball breaking away, and anticipating it next time.

Because the leg-break bowler, on a helpful wicket, can turn the ball a lot, and can turn it both ways, and can vary the amount of spin, the variety open to him is endless. He can vary his pace, use the crease, and if a left-handed batsman comes in he is well placed to exploit the rough worn outside the left-hander's off stump by the feet of previous bowlers.

Attacking Field

The leg spinner wants to encourage the batsman to play strokes and miscue. So if the wicket is helping him he will have men in catching positions on the offside, such as mid-off and extra cover, for the batsman who attempts to hit on the leg side against the spin. To encourage the batsman to do this he could well leave inviting gaps in the leg-side

field, tempting him to hit towards mid-wicket, say.

He'll need close-in catchers on both sides of the wicket for the bat-pad catch which results in an uncertain batsman prodding at the ball. A typical beg-break bowler's attacking field is in illustration 1.

Defensive Field

A leg-spinner will not be brought on to defend, but he may be put on when the batsmen are on top in an effort to 'buy' a wicket. His field will then have deeper catchers on the off side, as in illustration 2.

Marshall Law

■ As a leg-spinner, be philosophical. Things will not always go your way, and even the best sometimes pick up analyses of nought for plenty.
■ Field setting is more important to you than any other bowler. Do not be afraid to change your field often to take account of the success or miscues the batsmen are having. Learn as you play!

Bowling Left-Arm Spin

Marshall Law

■ Put plenty of zip in your action by bracing yourself and swivelling against your front leg. But don't become jerky. Power with smoothness is the aim.

■ Practise your line and length in the nets. Accuracy should be the strength of a left-arm spinner. Any deviations in length, especially pitching short, will be punished.

T HE left-arm spinner has a big advantage in cricket, where most of the batsmen are right-handed. He can bowl with finger-spin like an off-spinner does, and can command the same accuracy, but he has the bonus that his normal delivery leaves the batsman instead of coming in to him.

Strangely there are few left-hand spinners in the lists of record wicket-takers in Tests, the outstanding one being Derek Underwood, whose 297 wickets could have been more. And he was almost medium pace at times. Perhaps the next revival in bowling fashion will be the left-arm slow spinner.

Grip and Action

The grip (see photograph) is the same as for the off-spinner, with the first two fingers spaced wide apart and across the seam with the top joints of the two fingers gripping the seam. The third and fourth fingers help hold it in position, while the thumb rests lightly against it. It is the top joints of the first and second fingers, particularly the first finger, which imparts the spin. The action is the same as for the off-spinner, with everything reversed right to left.

Left-hander's Line

The usual technique for the left-arm bowler is to come round-the-wicket, keeping as close to the stumps as

1 The leap into the delivery stride, with a good lean back away from the batsman.

2 Into the delivery stride with the leading arm high and the head kept as still as possible.

3 The front leg coming down with the right arm pulling the body forward. The head remains still.

The grip for the orthodox left-arm slow bowler.

possible if the ball isn't turning much and perhaps going wider if the wicket is helpful. Keep the ball well pitched up to the batsman so that he will be tempted to reach for the pitch of the ball and will be punished for a misjudgement.

The ball will come into the batsman through the air, and if it pitches somewhere around middle and off it will at worst straighten, giving the bowler a chance for an lbw decision. If it turns more, a slip catch could result.

The front leg lands and the body pivot rounds. Note the stride is not long and the delivery high.

Derek Underwood of Kent and England, a left-armer who had almost perfect control over length, line and flight. There is probably plenty of turn in the wicket, as he is using the full width of the crease.

Left-Arm Spinners' Variations and Fields

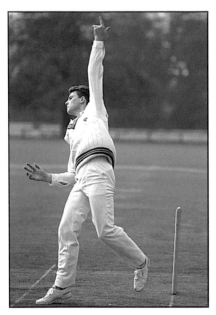

For the stock delivery the ball is delivered at the top of the swing.

THE left-arm spinner, because he uses the same methods as the off-spinner, has the same varieties of delivery open to him. But of course everything is in reverse – whereas the off-spinner's stock delivery moves into the batsman, the left-armer's moves away, and it is the left-armer's floater that moves into the batsman.

The Arm-ball

The left-hander bowls an arm-ball in the same manner as the off-spinner (see pages 36 and 37). Instead of holding its line towards the slips, as the off-breaker's arm-ball might, the left-armer's arm ball will come on towards the wicket. It is, in fact, more dangerous, because being of necessity bowled from a slightly wider angle, it spears in more and

By releasing the ball just before the top of the swing, the ball will be sent on a higher trajectory and will take longer to reach the batsman.

will either bowl the batsman or trap him lbw if he misjudges it. For this reason it is a good idea to bowl the arm-ball slightly quicker to force the batsman into being late with his reaction.

The Floater

Because the left-armer's arm-ball is already a lethal delivery as just

described, it would seem unnecessary for a left-armer to want to bowl the equivalent of the off-spinner's floater (see pages 36 and 37). However, there is no harm in being able to bowl this delivery, as anything which surprises the batsman is a good ball. You might get bat-pad catches at short leg with it.

Bowling to Left-handers

When bowling to a left-handed batsman, the left-arm bowler has the same circumstances as an off-spinner bowling to a right-hand batsman. In this case he might decide to go over the wicket, especially if there are rough patches outside the off-stump which he can take advantage of. It is only the presence of such rough which might encourage him to bowl over-the-wicket to a right-hander, but it is not something to be done unless desperate for a variation. It invites the batsman to pad away all the time.

By releasing the ball after the top of the swing, the ball will have a flatter trajectory and will be faster. The arm speed remains the same for all three balls to help deceive the batsman.

Chinaman

A Chinaman is described as a left-hander's googly, but since the orthodox left-hander is not a wrist spinner, there is some disagreement on what exactly is meant. For the left-arm spinner to bowl an off-break to a right-hander which is what is usually meant, he would have to employ the leg-break action of a right-arm bowler, and this seems somewhat pointless. Unless you can bowl a good wrist-spinner already, I suggest you don't bother!

Flight

Flight is the other main weapon of a left-hand spinner. By releasing the ball earlier or later in the delivery swing, the bowler can make the ball slightly faster or slower and its arc higher or lower than the stock delivery. This is not like the fast

Marshall Law

■ For a left-arm spinner, there is not the same benefit to be gained in varying the deliveries as there is for a fast bowler, say. When to vary the delivery is a battle of wits with the batsman. The ideal time is when the batsman is so sure he knows what the next delivery will do that he plays carelessly or attempts a risky shot. If you can make the ball do something different on that very delivery, you win the battle of minds.

bowler's slower ball, which is obviously different in speed – this is to deceive the batsman into thinking that the delivery is the same as the previous one (or half-dozen).

Unfortunately for him it turns out to be slightly different, and he can think about how different all the way back to the pavilion. There is more about flight on the following pages.

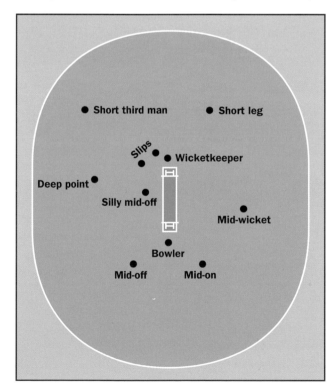

An attacking field for a left-arm spinner, bowling round the wicket.

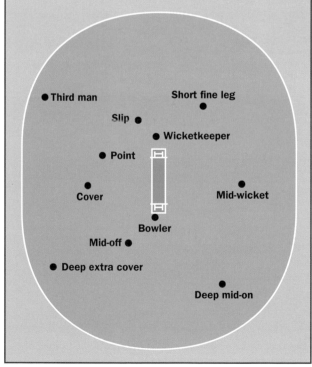

A defensive field for a left-arm spinner bowling round the wicket on an easy pitch.

Spinner's Length, Line and Flight

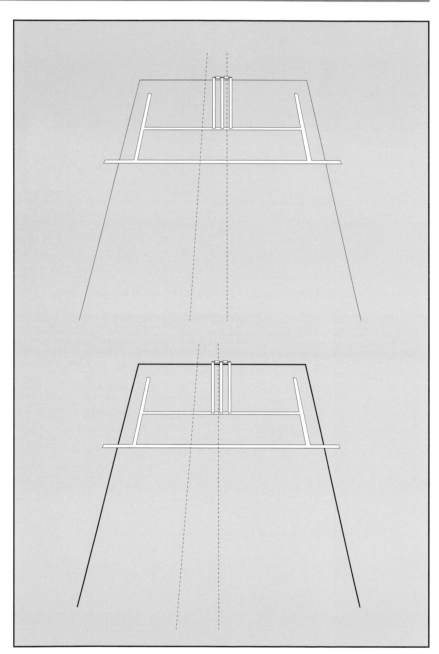

The off-spinner's standard line (bottom), on or just outside off-stump and the standard line for the leg-spinner or left-arm spinner (top), from middle to off-stump. The leg-spinner will bowl a few just outside off-stump to soften up the batsman for the googly. All spinners will vary their line tactically.

SPINNERS must get their line and length right or they will be punished. A batsman has plenty of time to hit a wayward ball if it is arriving slowly.

Length

The right length for a slow bowler is one which puts the batsman into two minds as to whether he goes forward or back. Ideally, he will think he can play forward, but when he does he discovers he should have played back, because he has been deceived about the pitch of the ball. So a full length is required – the sort of length where a batsman quick on his feet might try to make it a half-volley, and a more static batsman might prod forward hopefully.

Flight

Flight is the way the bowler can deceive a batsman about the ball's length. The principles were explained on the previous pages. The slower the bowler, the more part flight will play in his technique. Fast spinners will not use flight as much as slow bowlers like Richard Illingworth, the off-spinner who played against West Indies in 1991.

The way to vary the flight is to release the ball slightly earlier or later than usual (see the photographs on pages 44-45). Releasing the ball earlier will toss it higher into the air, and make it slightly slower and shorter in length. These variations must be subtle, so that the batsman plays as if he is receiving a normal delivery. The ball released later, of course, will be slightly quicker, fuller in pitch and flatter. The arm action and speed is the same.

The ball delivered with the quicker, flatter, flight could well be the arm-ball, the intention being to hurry the ball onto the batsman who, if he plays for the spin, will not have time to adjust.

The more flighted ball should be spun harder than normal, as the spin could make it dip in flight, thus helping even more to ensure that the batsman who is tempted forward might find the ball isn't where he expects it (see illustration below). Even for an already slow bowler, the slower ball might be one of his most profitable.

The important thing is that each delivery should look the same to the batsman. The subtleties of flight are all about disguise.

Line

The line a spinner bowls will depend on what the wicket is doing and the state of the match.

The off-spinner's standard line will be on or just outside the off-stump, allowing the turning ball to hit the wicket. Only in a one-day match or if there is a need to bowl defensively will an off-spinner switch to bowling at the middle and leg stumps with a packed leg-side field.

The leg-break bowler and the orthodox left-arm spinner will bowl more to the leg than the off-spinner because their stock ball is moving away from the batsman – their line will be middle to off stump. They are

Marshall Law

■ Keep attacking, especially if you are learning your trade. An off-spinner who spears the ball at the batsman's leg stump with a low trajectory might concede fewer runs than if he flighted the ball, and a Test captain might order such tactics in certain circumstances, but it is not something the up-and-coming spinner should practise.

■ Practise your line and length by placing a page from a newspaper or a large handkerchief on the relevant spot when in the nets – but only if it's not windy!

not always trying to hit the stumps, but to get snicks to slip. More attacking bowlers might bowl further to leg, so that most deliveries will hit the stumps, but anything which pitches outside leg stump is usually a mistake. I say 'usually' because I remember how Shane Warne bowled Mike Gatting with a ball which turned 18 inches – it was his first ball in an Ashes Test match. Rough outside the leg stump is a temptation to a leg-spinner to pitch here.

All spinners will alter their line when bowling to left-handers, of course. An off-spinner will probably go round the wicket and bowl at middle and off stump. The leg-break and left-arm bowler will pitch on or outside off-stump, particularly if there is rough there. The leg-breaker in particular has the chance to make the ball break a long way and the poor left-hander is unable to pad up safely – he always risks getting an lbw decision against him.

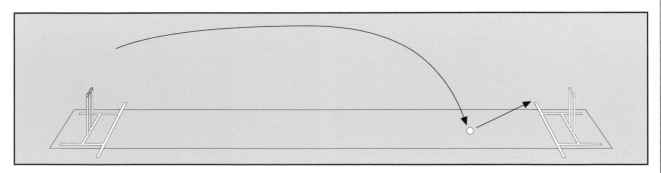

A flighted ball with plenty of spin will dip late in its flight. If it is of the length shown, the batsman will be tempted forward and will find the ball isn't as far up to him as he thought, and will have to adjust quickly.

Bowling in One-Day Games

BOWLING in one-days games is a little different in that the main aim is to keep the runs down rather than take wickets. Personally I think getting the batsman out is the best way to restrict his scoring, and batsmen find accurate, hostile, fast bowling difficult to score from anyway, so it doesn't make as much difference to me as to a slower bowler, perhaps. But all bowlers have to contend with the restrictions on field placings, and must bowl to their fields. And the captain will soon have a word to say if runs are given away unnecessarily.

Fast bowling

At the beginning of the innings the fast bowler will want to get wickets, so will have a couple of slips and a gully, his most productive area for catches. He will keep the ball up and on or outside off stump. He will need a third man, deep on the fence to cut off the fours which can easily result from a snick, a fine leg on the boundary and some other men deepish on the leg side, too. A mid-on and mid-off will save the bowler from having to chase the ball from those firm shots past the bowler.

Medium-pace Seam Bowling

Much of the middle part of a one-day innings these days, particularly in England, is taken up with medium-pace bowlers bowling seamers. By now the batsmen will be starting to push the score along, and the seam bowler will not want more than the necessary five fielders (including the wicket-keeper) inside the statutory circle. His field might well spread out, as illustrated in the diagram below left.

Off-spin Bowling

Off-spinners in one-day cricket will probably be encouraged to attack the middle and leg stumps with a 6-3 leg-side field. Three men will parade the ropes for the lofted drive or hook (see diagram below right). The custom these days is for captains to

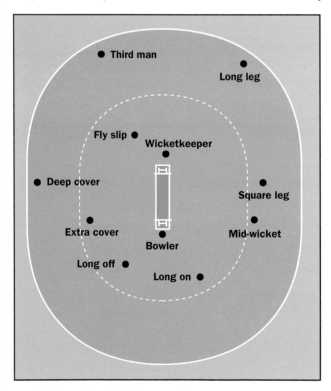

A typical one-day field for a medium-pace seam bowler, designed to keep the runs down.

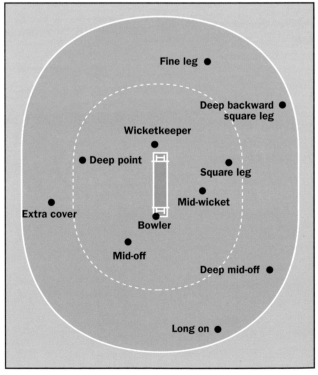

An off-spinner's one-day field, with most fielders on the leg-side as he bowls on the middle and leg stumps.

Kent bowling to Middlesex at Lord's in an AXA Equity & Law one-day game have five fielders within the circle.

bowl spinners in the middle of the innings, usually each side of an interval, when batsmen are least likely to cut loose.

Left-Arm Slow Bowling

Left-arm slow bowlers will also concentrate on leg and middle stumps, but because they turn away from the batsman, who might 'make room' anyway, their leg-side field will be 5-4. If they prefer an orthodox line on middle and off stumps, a 5-4 off-side field will be required with a square leg, perhaps, moving across to the off-side.

Slow bowlers need not be expensive in one-day cricket. Batsmen cannot use the pace of the ball in making shots, and must generate their own power. Clever field-placing can get them out.

Marshall Law

■ In one-day cricket the onus is on the batsman to score, so if you can block off his more productive strokes he will start getting anxious and might try something rash.

■ Be aware of the ebbs and flows and nuances of one-day cricket. A couple of overs with the wrong field, or bowling down the wrong line, could give away a critical number of runs before you realise it.

■ Take care that you and the captain are on the same wavelength and you both agree on what you're trying to do.

Fielding

IN THE old days nobody thought too much about fielding. The portly older players could be put in the slips where they wouldn't have to run about too much, while the youngsters were given the task of chasing round the boundary. Outfielders were expected to bend down to stop the ball with their hand rather than their foot, but they certainly weren't expected to dive. In some quarters, that sort of thing would be seen as 'not quite cricket'.

The one-day game certainly altered all that. Nowadays all first-class cricketers – well, practically all – are expected to be fit and agile. It became apparent that in a one-day game a good fielder could save perhaps 20 runs. Multiply the fielders by ten and the one day by five and you can appreciate how many runs fielders can save in a Test match. All right – I know that means Test matches could end in a 'no-score draw', but you know what I mean. I remember my first season in England in 1979 when, incidentally, I picked up a World Cup winner's medal without playing in any of the games. I was the best rewarded drinks waiter in the world! I particularly remember the final, when England won the toss and put us in at Lord's. When he had scored nine, Gordon Greenidge was brilliantly run out by Derek Randall. Randall's fielding has been celebrated the world over, but how many runs was that piece of inspired action worth? In the semi-final against Pakistan Greenidge and Haynes had opened with 132 – now they fell 110 runs short of that. Greenidge had averaged 122 up to the final, so did Randall's fielding brilliance save his side 113 runs from Greenidge? Should that be added to his own score?

That's not a serious question, of course, but it is a shame that while batsmen and bowlers have aggregates and averages and everybody can see their worth over a game, a season or a career, fielders don't get such recognition.

Everybody knows who the good fielders are, of course, and their value to the side is well recognised. In the West Indies we all know how many runs Clive Lloyd, Viv Richards and Roger Harper, for example, have saved for us by their catching and stopping, and all the other countries have their outstanding fielders.

The Importance of Good Fielding

When you come to think of it, a batsman would virtually have to carry his bat through every match he played to spend as much time at the crease as in the field, and even the best bowler cannot bowl more than half the overs in an innings, so must field for much longer than he bowls. In all, a cricketer probably spends at

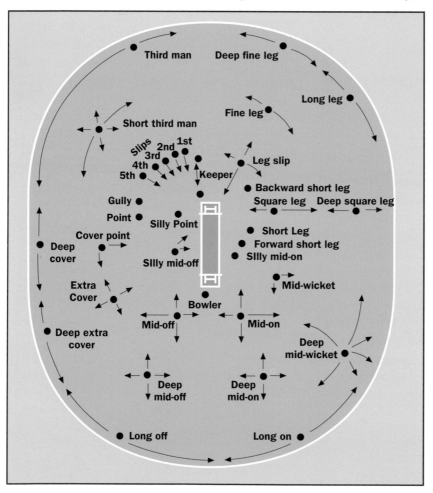

Learn what the terms are for positions on the field. These are for a right-handed batsman. They are not fixed positions and can all be moved by the standard qualifications like 'squarer', 'finer', 'deeper', 'shorter', etc.

least three-quarters of his active cricket life fielding! So it is essential to take it seriously, practise hard and to be at least adequate at it.

The run saving value of good fielding has already been touched upon, but just as important is its psychological value, both positively for your teammate the bowler, and negatively for the batsman. A bowler can be lifted by the knowledge that his fielders are backing him up, that the catches are being caught and the runs saved. And the batsman, who finds his best strokes are not bringing him the runs he feels he deserves, gets frustrated and is inclined to take more risks.

Bad fielding has the opposite effect, of course. The bowler is discouraged if his best work goes unrewarded, while the batsman's

A piece of fielding brilliance from Derek Randall in the 1979 World Cup Final at Lord's puts paid to Gordon Greenidge's dreams of another century.

confidence soars if he finds runs are coming without too much effort.

Concentration and Alertness

The fielding skills are catching, running, picking up and throwing. Some players will naturally be more gifted than others. But all should do their best, and this involves 100 per cent concentration and alertness. It sounds an easy requirement: concentration. But it isn't, especially if the fielding stint lasts for six hours or more, as it does in a Test match.

It might sound strange, but concentration and alertness come more easily if you're fit. Even standing at slip with hardly a snick coming your way is very tiring. You still have to be on your toes every ball, because the next one could easily be the one that brings you a catch.

Specialisation

Slip fielding is a specialised position, and there are players who have built reputations as superb fieldsmen on nothing more than slip-catching. I would not worry too much about specialisation early in a career – you will doubtless be asked to field in all sorts of places, anyway. In time you and your colleagues will get to know where you can be most useful.

To start with, if you are a fast runner and good thrower, you might want to prowl the boundary. If you pride yourself on lightning reflexes you might fancy the slips – even short leg, probably the most unpopular position on the field. If you are a bowler you might think third man or fine leg is a place where you can rest between overs – although it doesn't always work out like that. If you are quick and enjoy fielding, and want to test yourself

Throughout my career I have practised my fielding, and know I have played my part in the team effort.

against the batsman in the widest and most active way, you might field in the covers, where great fielders like Hobbs, Bradman, Neil Harvey and Clive Lloyd have excelled.

Whatever your fancy – it is better to practise your weaknesses than settle for your strengths. And as you improve as a fielder, the more you will get like those cover-points just mentioned, and enjoy it.

Marshall Law

■ There is no excuse for not doing your best as a fielder. To claim to be a 'batsman' or a 'bowler' and to go through the motions of fielding is just not good enough.
■ Fitness equals concentration equals better fielding. So get fit to field!
■ Unless you're weak at it, fielding is fun, so practise and get better. You'll spend a long time doing it every match, anyway.

Fielding in the Deep

THE first requirement of a fielder fielding round the boundary is to

1

The ball is arriving and I have got behind the line and am dropping into the long barrier position.

stop the ball going for four or six runs. Catching is dealt with in the following pages, so these pages will deal with ground fielding.

A fielder on the boundary can walk in a little as the bowler is running up in order to get himself on his toes and ready to move fast, but the boundary fielder mustn't overdo this. He has been put on the boundary because the bowler and/or captain expect, or hope, that the batsman will hit the ball hard in that direction, perhaps in the air. If the fielder comes in too far, and the ball sails over his head, he will be in trouble all round.

But he has to be ready and concentrating, and he must watch the batsman all through his stoke to try to anticipate the direction the ball will be hit. At the time of the stroke, he will be loose and balanced, ready

2

I am in position with both hands behind the ball and the right foot and slightly overlapping left knee forming a second line of defence. Note the head over the ball.

to sprint towards the line of the ball. His body will be slightly bent towards the batsman, and his arms will be loose.

As soon as the ball is hit, the fielder will want to pick up the line as quickly as possible, and he must use his judgement to decide where he can intercept the ball. Obviously, it should be as near to the wicket as possible. He wants to prevent the

batsman taking a second or third run and if the opportunity arises to get a run-out. He runs as quickly as possible to his target.

The Long Barrier

Once at the ball, he must get down to stop it. Unless there is the prospect of a run-out, and especially if the surface is uneven for any reason, the safest way to stop the ball is by means of the 'long barrier'. This is a barrier formed by one foot and the opposite knee. For example, if the ball is coming to your right-hand side you should get down to stop the ball with your right foot and left knee forming the barrier, as in

3

Rising with the ball in both hands, but transferring it to the right hand.

the photographs. Don't take the ball too far back on your left leg.

For a right-handed thrower, the ball coming to the right is easy, the picking up and throwing being natural. If the ball is coming to the left, however, you have to make a choice. If there is time, the fielder can run round and field in the same manner. If there isn't time, then the fielder must form the long barrier with his left foot and right knee, and must pivot on his right foot as he rises to step forward with his left foot into the throwing position.

The fielder must get down early and take the ball with his head still and over the ball. It is important to keep your eye on the ball until it is safely into your hands. Taking your eye off the ball and starting the next move before the ball is safely gathered in is the way misfields happen.

Use both hands to stop the ball wherever possible.

Throwing in

Throwing in should be to the wicket keeper, unless there is a good chance of a run-out at the bowler's end. The pick-up and throw is a natural

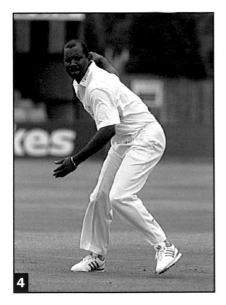

4

4. The right arm is moving back to throw while the left leg begins its step forward.

movement from the long barrier fielding position as in the photographs. The right foot will already be square i.e. at right angles to the wicket, and as you rise with your

Marshall Law

■ Use your head when fielding, and not only to think with. When you gather the ball it should be still and over the ball.
■ Watch the batsman's movements, particularly his feet. The way he shapes to play the ball will give you a good idea of where it will go.
■ Keep your eyes on the ball

weight on this foot and transfer the ball to your right hand, the left leg can step forward ready to throw. The right arm, with elbow bent and wrist cocked, moves back to throw while the left arm stretches out towards the target to act as a guide. As the weight transfers to the left foot, the throwing arm straightens and throws. The ball should be aimed full toss to arrive just over the bails, or if you are too far out, to arrive first bounce.

5

5. A quick but powerful throw to the wicketkeeper.

By the way, if the ball is swinging a lot, the grip shown on page 20 to prevent the ball swinging can also be used to throw in to the wicket-keeper – the ball will not swing so much.

Using the Foot and Sliding

Believe it or not, it was once thought 'not the thing' to stop the ball with the foot. Nowadays we consider that anything that works is perfectly OK, and a fielder chasing round the boundary who cannot get down to use his hands is perfectly in order to stop the ball with his foot. In fact he'll be out of order if he just lets it pass.

Present-day cricketers have gone beyond this, however. It is quite common now to see players slide into the ropes, knocking the ball back with a hand and recovering to save a run. I have one reservation about this otherwise admirable show of athleticism and enthusiasm. If you are your team's principal bowler, putting yourself out of action for a spell by getting injured while saving one run is not a good bargain for your side. Use a bit of discretion!

Catching in the Deep

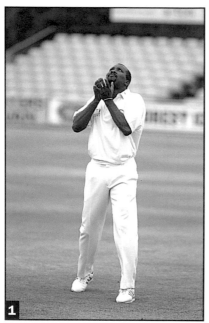

1

Getting ready to make a conventional catch, eyes on the ball, hands ready to take the ball just in front of the chin.

POSITIONING is the most important aspect of catching in the deep. Most catches are missed, particularly in the skier category, because the fielder hasn't quite got into the right position.

The first essential is not to commit yourself too early. By all means move in the general direction of the ball – for instance if the line is clearly to your left, move that way – but be careful not to rush in too quickly. On the previous pages I mentioned you should not be moving

in from the boundary as the ball is bowled, and this is one reason why you shouldn't. It is much easier to catch the ball if you are running in towards it, and we see quite a lot of quite spectacular catches taken on the run in this way. But if you come in too soon, and have to move back, it is much more difficult.

If the ball is coming high, your first objective is to get underneath it. You should position yourself so that the ball arrives just in front of you. You take it at somewhere around

2

Fingers spread, I am just about to take the ball at the base of my fingers.

throat height (see photographs 1-3). This is the conventional method. Your hands should be spread wide to form a large cup for the ball to fall into, the fingers out straight. The ball should land at the base of the fingers which should close round it.

You should watch the ball all the way into your hands, consistent with keeping your head still. And as the ball makes contact with the hands,

you should let the hands give a little, i.e. move downwards with the ball. This gives the ball less opportunity to bounce out, and it also cushions the impact and doesn't hurt your hands. It shouldn't hurt if you catch the ball correctly – it is the mistimed ones which sting. If you allow the hands and arms to give you should be able to bring your hands close in to your chest to complete the catch.

The More Lateral Catch

If the ball is coming to you flatter but will still arrive at or above your head, the technique is to reverse the hands so that the fingers point upwards, the thumbs touching and

3

My fingers have closed round the ball and the hands have given slightly to rest against my chest.

the palms facing the ball. The catch should be completed just to one side of the head, and the natural give will take the ball just past your ear. In the second sequence of photographs I am using this technique but the ball is still dropping, so I have my fingers pointing backwards and upwards rather than upwards only. The ball is landing very slightly to one side of my face, which makes it easy to keep my eyes on the ball, and the give takes the ball comfortably towards my shoulder.

This technique can actually be used for all catches, including skiers. I prefer the conventional method, but you will find Australians using the fingers upwards technique for all catches. It's just the way they've been brought up.

Of course even in the deep you might have to dive or jump and use one or two hands to make the catch – these are more like the close-to-the wicket catches which are dealt with later.

Legal and Illegal Catches

Few people know exactly what the laws allow when making a catch on the boundary. A catch is legal if you

Marshall Law

■ If you practise catching high balls in the deep, you will find that you will not have to make a conscious decision as to whether to catch the ball with little fingers together or thumbs together, it will come naturally to you.
■ Make sure you don't run in too fast and over-run the ball. It is far easier to make a catch with the ball dropping in front of you than behind you.
■ Really, the key to catching in the deep is confidence. If you expect to catch it, the chances are you will. Practise so that you know you will make the catch, and banish all those doubts which lead other more timid people to miss them.

do not touch or ground any part of your person on or over a boundary line. If the boundary line is a rope, you cannot therefore have a foot on or over it. Where there is a fence, however, you are allowed to touch the fence or use it as a support as you lean over it, but you must not touch the ground on the other side with any part of your body.

In this sequence the ball is arriving on a flatter trajectory, and I have reversed my hands so that the palms are outwards, thumbs touching.

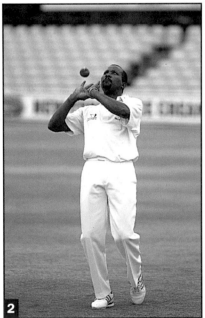

The ball is about to land at the base of my fingers. With all catches it is important to watch the ball right into the hands.

I have allowed the hands and arms to give with the ball and have finished with my hands just below my shoulder.

Going for the Run-Out

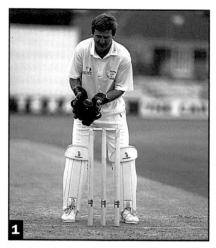

1

The ideal place for a wicketkeeper to take the throw. Bobby Parks, my Hampshire 'keeper for over 200 matches, gets the ball just above the bails.

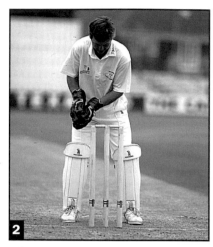

2

With the minimum of movement ...

THE best all-round fielders in a side often choose cover-point or extra cover as their position, because this usually affords the best chance of a run-out. Mid-wicket and square leg are other positions where good anticipation, agile fielding and a fast and accurate throw can often cause a run-out. These fielders will usually be placed close enough to the wicket to 'save the single' but far enough out for them to cover as wide an arc as possible to stop the boundaries. This is why these positions are so challenging. Whenever the batsman plays the ball into the covers, say, wide of the fielder, there is always the chance of a single but always the

chance of a run-out if the batsmen hesitate. Players like Clive Lloyd and Derek Randall saved many singles just by being there – they inhibited the batsmen who decided that discretion was the better part of valour.

If I take fielding in the covers as typical of this position, I would say

the first requirement of the fielder is to be ready to spring into action as the ball is played. This is why the gentle walk inward as the ball is bowled is recommended. When the shot is played the fielder is already on the move, on his toes, loose of limb and hands at the ready.

The second requirement is anticipation. The fielder should watch the batsman's movements closely. His feet will give early indication of

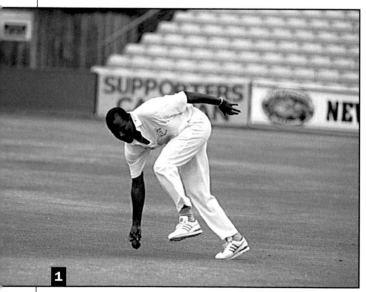

1

I am picking up the ball one-handed in full flight, having judged that there is a possibility of a run-out.

2

You can see from the advertising hoardings that my throwing arm is moving back in the same stride.

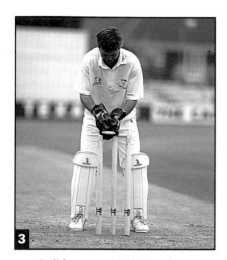

... a bail is removed. And so is another unlucky batsman.

ball will be picked up and thrown, as the commentators say, 'in the same movement'.

What often goes wrong here is at the crucial moment the fielder takes his eye off the ball because he is too aware of the position of the wicket and the batsman running towards it. How often do you see run-out situations on the television where you watch closely the batsman and the wicket in an attempt to pre-empt the umpire's finger only to find the stumps stay undisturbed. Looking back you find the fielder did everything else right, but he failed to gather the ball.

Keep your eye on the ball till it is in the hand. As you pick it up you take your arm back ready to throw and only then do your eyes look up at the target. This may be the stumps themselves if unattended, or the wicketkeeper or fielder guarding them.

In either case the throw should be immediate and fast. Accuracy is sometimes sacrificed – but then this is what sorts out the great fielders from the merely good ones. The

his intentions and some guide as to where he will play the ball. The best fielders, like the best batsmen, pick up the line of the ball quickly and accelerate to the point where they will stop it.

Picking up the ball when attempting a run-out in these circumstances will not be as elaborate as for the long barrier described earlier. The fielding will be accomplished one-handed and the

Marshall Law

■ Alertness and concentration are what's needed in the 'run-out' positions. In another word, keenness. The best cover fieldsmen are those who are good, know they're good, and enjoy making life hell for the batsmen.
■ A fast reaction time gets wickets. And that comes from being ready to pounce at every ball.
■ Don't get excited too soon. Keep your eye on the ball and start celebrating only when the batsman is walking back to the pavilion.

quickest throw is the flat one from just below the shoulders. It should hit the stumps or whistle into the wicketkeeper's gloves near the bails – ideally just above them.

As my right leg comes forward I am poised to throw and have switched my eyes to the target.

I have thrown the ball flat from just below the shoulder with my weight on the right foot.

Fielding Close to the Wicket

CLOSE fielders are mainly there to pick up catches. They do not need the running and throwing power of other fielders; rather they need super-concentration and lightning reflexes.

The two main kinds of close fielders are the slips, where the ball comes to them from a snick, and the short legs and silly points, etc, where the ball might pop up at an unexpected angle from the bat or bat and pad.

Slip Fielding

Slip fielders should stand in a comfortable and balanced position on the balls of the feet, which should be about 2 feet (60 centimetres) apart. The knees should be bent and the body leaning forward, the hands held slightly apart, fingers pointing downwards and palms towards the batsman. The head should remain still, with the eyes level.

In this position you are ready to sway, or even to dive, to the left, right or even to some extent forward to make the catch. If the ball is low, you are already there. If it is high, your half-crouch helps you rise quickly to take the catch. You watch the ball right into your hands, which should be allowed to give a little so that the ball doesn't bounce out.

It is imperative that you stay in your half-crouch until you see the ball from the bat. The reason for this is that it is much easier to get up for the higher catches then to get down for the low ones. So you should not begin to rise as the ball approaches the batsman, which is a common fault with young cricketers.

It is best for first slip to watch the ball all the way, as the wicketkeeper does, for any snick to him will be a very slight one. The other slips will probably find it easier to concentrate on watching the bat. The fielder at the far end of the slip cordon, gully, will get the ball from a very thick edge, or even a genuine cut, so he *must* watch the bat (and be prepared for stinging hands from time to time).

Concentration (Again!)

Concentration is vital for the slips. You might stand at slip for 600 deliveries or so during a day's fielding, and from those only a dozen or so times might the ball come in your direction. But if two of those are catches, whether you catch them or not could make the difference between winning and losing the match. Slip fielders tend to keep their concentration by chatting and stretching between deliveries and switching their concentration on again as the bowler runs up for the next ball. One thing is certain: if you cannot prepare yourself stringently for action 600 times a day when you know that in, say, 580 cases you're wasting your time, then don't be a slip.

Short Legs

The other close positions – short leg, silly point, silly mid-off and mid-on, etc. – are different. And the main difference, to my mind at least, is that they are dangerous! Indeed you could almost say that the most important skill a fielder in these positions has to know is how to get out of the way. If a batsman cuts, drives, hooks or pulls straight at you, it does not do you or your side any

The batsman has gone too far down the wicket and I have got the ball away to the wicketkeeper in no time. If it doesn't hit the stumps my friend Mr Parks will do the necessary.

A fine run-out at the bowler's end. Graham Gooch, who is just out of picture at mid-on, hits the middle stump to run out India's Sharma for 38 and win the Lord's Test of 1990.

good if you are badly injured.

So I say to everybody asked to field in these positions: wear a helmet, and as much other protective gear as you can.

To talk of the positive first: what you are there for is to catch the ball from a prod or a snick from bat onto pad. So many of the remarks made about slips apply: you should be half-crouching on the balls of the feet ready to pounce left, right or upwards if necessary. Short-legs often find it best to get down very low. Clearly you cannot watch the bowler, and must watch the bat.

The batsman's foot movements and the swing of the bat will give you an early indication of what he intends to do, and if it is smash the ball in your direction you must take evasive action. On the off side, the best method is to turn your back and jump, because the ball will usually be played down to where your feet are. If you are on the leg side, however, your best bet is to stay down and turn your back on the batsman, making yourself as small as possible. This is because the pulls and hooks are often at head height. In all cases protect your head and face with your hands and arms.

The Under-Arm Run-Out

Close fielders sometimes have the chance of a run-out, usually if the batsman moves out of his ground as if to run and then goes back. The close fielder must always be alert for such chances and will have to take them instinctively. Since the fielding is usually done close to the ground the throw is underhand, often without any backswing. Practise hitting the wicket, or at least the wicketkeeper if he is standing up, from such situations.

Marshall Law

■ Constant concentration is the hallmark of the close fielder. You can't afford to concentrate only most of the time. If you miss a catch the next one could be a long time coming. And if you're still worrying about the first one, you'll miss the second one, too.

■ Close fielders in front of or square to the bat must stand their ground and not retreat when the batsman is making his stroke. But do not be foolishly brave. You must take evasive action when necessary. No catch is worth a serious injury.

Clothes, Nets, Fitness

YOU might think it a liberty if I mention clothes, but clothes are very important to a cricketer. It is not only a question of looking good leading to feeling good leading to playing well. There are some practical considerations as well.

For example, shirts should be loose-fitting, especially round the shoulders and armpits. It's not a bad idea to buy a size larger than you need for normal wear. You want freedom for your arms. Personally, I prefer short-sleeved shirts if the weather isn't too cold, and I must admit when I first came to play regularly in England it was. I prefer cotton shirts, too, because those with too much artificial fabric in them can get very sticky in hot weather. If you're a fast bowler, too, and therefore perspire quite a lot (we all know it's hard work) it might be as well to have a supply of vests to stop you cooling down too much between overs. You are probably bursting in at high speed for three or four minutes and then spending three or four standing still at long leg or somewhere. The man who invented the sauna bath was probably a fast bowler.

Sweaters, too, are important for the same reason, and in England in particular they will need to be of the long-sleeved variety for fielding between overs.

You should take great care over your boots or shoes. They must fit perfectly, for nothing is worse than bowling and fielding for a long day in ill-fitting footwear. It is impossible to give of your best if your feet are uncomfortable. And make sure your spikes are fitted properly and are secure. Think about socks, too. A fast bowler bangs his feet in quite hard (unless he's 'whispering' Michael Holding) and some players like to wear two pairs.

Trousers, too, should fit well. They should not be too baggy round the seat or too loose round the waist, and shouldn't be too long in the leg,

Net practice should be good constructive practice undertaken for a purpose, and not just turning the arm over for the sake of it. Decide what it is you want to achieve before you arrive, and then achieve it.

but at the same time they should not restrict your movement in any way.

On a sunny day you want some head protection, and a shade for the eyes. I quite like the wide-brimmed sun hat, but this is purely personal.

Net Practice

Net practice is vital. It gives you the chance to iron out faults you might have detected in your action. I use videos a lot to check on mine, particularly if I'm having a lean spell, but I appreciate it's much easier for me to do this than it is for the young club player. If there is nobody to film your action, the next best thing is to have a qualified coach or a trusted team-mate to give you their views on whether you have incorporated any faults. I put markers down to work at my length and line.

Don't forget to work at your strengths as well as your weaknesses in the nets. Don't let your good techniques go rusty. But if you are having problems with your technique at any time you need to have a coach with you at net practice to spot your faults.

Net practice also has the benefit of bringing the team together and fostering team spirit. One of the things you can practise together is catching, although this is not done in the nets themselves. Outfield catching practice can be achieved by a batsman hitting high balls towards a fielder with varying trajectories and fielding practice can be performed in the same way. The wicket-keeper joins in as the fielder throws in hard to him.

Slip fielders can practise on a catching cradle but some players prefer to have a batsman playing the ball to a line of slips for more realism. However even this can become predictable, just like the slip

cradle. You can try other variations, like throwing the ball at a roller (don't upset the groundsman) so that it comes off at different angles.

If you can invent games at net practice I am all for it, because the main thing about net practice is that it should be constructive and you should enjoy it. If you know what you want to practise, and set about it in an organised manner, and have some method of measuring your improvement, then you are achieving something. Carl Hooper is good at net practice. He is always keen and his enthusiasm is infectious.

If you go along to net practice because the captain ordered it, and you regard it as a chore to get through, then you'd be better off improving your fitness by running round the block.

Fitness

Which brings us to the last topic, keeping fit. The days when cricket was a game for toffs and getting fit was regarded as a sort of cheating are long gone. If you want to do well you've got to be fit, just as you have to be for football or any other competitive sport.

If your body is constantly working but not being strengthened it must break down. Why do so many English bowlers, particularly fast bowlers, break down? I think it is because the English season calls for cricket almost every day. The bowler is constantly working without the time to build up the muscles, and of course the variable English weather means he is bowling in hot weather one day, cold the next, damp the next and so on. It is like having a wooden house which withstands all weathers – but it needs painting and weather treatment and care or it will

'break down'. The wooden buildings at Hampshire's ground at Southampton have not weathered perfectly – one of the reasons why the club has been planning a move for some time.

I train often. 'Rest and strengthen' is my motto. I pay attention to hamstring, back, shoulder and abdominal muscles particularly. I have said earlier that in my view the abdominal muscles hold the secret to fast bowling. Potential fast bowlers, take note! I do plenty of sit-ups to strengthen my abdominals – 150 a day in batches of ten.

To sum up – keep fit, practise efficiently and have luck, and you will become a cricketer. All the best!

Malcolm Marshall's World XI

Malcom Marshall's Best Team

1	Gordon Greenidge	8	Richard Hadlee
2	Sunil Gavaskar	9	Andy Roberts
3	David Gower	10	Dennis Lillee
4	Viv Richards	11	Abdul Qadir
5	Allan Border		
6	Clive Lloyd (Capt.)	**12th Man**	
7	Rodney Marsh		Ian Botham

I HAVE picked my world's best team from players I have played with or against in my Test match career. There's no point in me giving you my opinion of W.G. Grace or Don Bradman, or even my hero Gary Sobers, whose last Test match was five years before my first. So here goes.

At number one, I would pick Gordon Greenidge, born seven years before me in Barbados and who like me played for Barbados, Hampshire and West Indies. Few opening batsmen hit the ball as hard as Gordon, and he was always on the attack from the first over. He had all the shots. He was superb in the seasons around 1984, and I remember in particular his 214 not out on the last day at Lord's when he led West Indies to their target of 342 to beat England. Gordon never allowed an innings to get bogged down – he could have a match half-won on the first day.

To open with Gordon I choose Sunny Gavaskar. His record speaks for itself: he was the first man to score 10,000 Test match runs. Of these, 774 came in his first series – in the West Indies. Four Tests, four centuries, average 154.80 – not bad for a 21-year-old. India won the series, too. It was the start of a long Test career for the 'Little Master', who ended with an average over 50.

At number three, I want David Gower – and this is not just to provide 'elegance' and look good. As one of those who had to try to get him out, I can tell you his was one of the most difficult wickets to take. His eye and his timing were superb.

Nothing disheartens a bowler more than when his best deliveries are sent seemingly effortlessly to the boundary. There was nothing really effortless about David's batting, of course. It all takes practice. In the West Indies we have the highest regard for his application and graft.

At number four would have to be Viv Richards, a man I have enjoyed watching as he took the best bowling sides apart all round the world. I loved bowling against him – but not because I found him easy to get out! It was a pleasure to see a master at work at the other end. I haven't seen anybody bat more naturally than Viv – when he was on form it seemed that he could do whatever he liked with whatever was bowled at him.

Allan Border is my number five. He is another with a long career and he now leads the list of Test run-makers, but it is the manner in which he scored his runs that I like. So often Allan has had the whole weight of Australian expectations on his shoulders and he has battled through with great character to achieve his record.

All the players I've picked so far have captained a Test side, but the man I would have to lead my world eleven would be Clive Lloyd, coming in at number six. Clive was the skipper who really got the West Indies buzzing in the 1970s. He was also a great attacking batsman and a superb fielder.

As wicketkeeper-batsman at number seven, I choose Rodney Marsh. He triumphed after a poorish start to his Test career, when he was nicknamed 'Old Irongloves', because the ball kept bouncing out of them. It shows what determination can do that he finished with a record 355 Test victims. He took 95 catches

The captain of my World XI would be the man who captained me in many Tests – Clive Lloyd of West Indies.

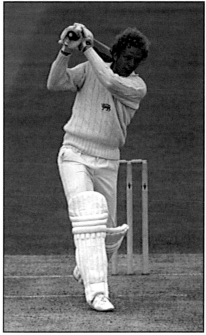

Another left-hander and another colleague, but only in my last seasons at Hampshire – David Gower.

Continuing the Hampshire theme, one of my World XI fast bowlers would be Andy Roberts of Antigua.

(another record) from Dennis Lillee's bowling – so I want him to hang on to the snicks in my team. He was also a useful left-handed batsman, who scored 3,633 runs in his 96 Test matches.

Of the bowling battery, Richard Hadlee will go in at number eight, possibly higher, because he is a genuine all-rounder, with 3,124 Test runs to his name, as well as his world record 431 Test wickets. He is, coincidentally, the fifth left-handed batsman in my team – and a very aggressive one at that. He is everything I admire in a fast bowler, with a model action and attitude. He topped the bowling averages in five out of eight English seasons in the 1980s, and was second in two of the other three

Andy Roberts comes next – like Hadlee a deep thinker about fast bowling. He followed Greenidge to Hampshire, and I followed him.

Andy really began the upsurge in West Indian fast bowling in the 1970s, and all of us since owe a lot to him. He and Richards both come from the small Caribbean island of Antigua.

At ten is Dennis Lillee, and no fast bowlers in the world will dispute this choice, for we all rate Dennis. He overcame back trouble to become the world's leading fast bowler in the early 1970s. Again, his action is a model for young players, as is his courage and application.

For a spinner I include Abdul Qadir, the Pakistani leg-spinner and general bamboozler. I remember him getting six for 16 when West Indies were bowled out for their lowest Test score of 53 at Faisalabad in 1986-87. He has consistently baffled the best batsmen for a long time.

My twelfth man is Ian Botham, because he was a cricketer capable of anything and could stand in if any of

my team were injured, except perhaps Abdul Qadir. Ian is one of those players who make things happen, a valuable asset in any side. And he's good for morale!

Now comes the realisation of all the great players I've left out. I could start again at the top and list another twelve men, starting at number one with Geoffrey Boycott, a batsman I've always admired. His wicket was always the most prized for any bowler. At number two . . . but if I carry on I will have picked two world elevens.

The most serious omission is, of course, M.D. Marshall – because if in 100 years time this team was put together in heaven to play for my particular cricketing era, I'd want to be in it! So Richard, Andy and Dennis: watch out that you don't get an accidental kick on your ankle just hard enough to make you cry off for the big match.

Index